LEARN MORE PYTHON 3
THE HARD WAY

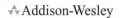

LEARN MORE PYTHON 3 THE HARD WAY

The Next Step for New Python Programmers

Zed A. Shaw

✦✦ Addison-Wesley

Boston • Columbus • Indianapolis • New York • San Francisco • Amsterdam • Cape Town
Dubai • London • Madrid • Milan • Munich • Paris • Montreal • Toronto • Delhi • Mexico City
São Paulo • Sydney • Hong Kong • Seoul • Singapore • Taipei • Tokyo

For information about buying this title in bulk quantities, or for special sales opportunities (which may include electronic versions; custom cover designs; and content particular to your business, training goals, marketing focus, or branding interests), please contact our corporate sales department at corpsales@pearsoned.com or (800) 382-3419.

For government sales inquiries, please contact governmentsales@pearsoned.com.

For questions about sales outside the U.S., please contact intlcs@pearson.com.

Visit us on the Web: informit.com/aw

Library of Congress Control Number: 2017946529

ISBN-13: 978-0-13-412348-6
ISBN-10: 0-13-412348-4

1 17

Contents

Preface

P rocess, creativity, and quality. Burn these three words into your mind while you read this book. Process. Creativity. Quality. This book may be full of exercises that teach important topics every programmer should know, but the real knowledge you'll gain from the book is these three words. My goal in writing this book on programming is to teach you what I've known to be the three most important constants in software. Without process you'll flounder around wondering how to get started and have problems maintaining progress on long projects. Without creativity you'll be unable to solve the problems you'll encounter every day as a programmer. Without quality you'll have no idea if anything you're doing is any good.

Teaching you these three concepts is easy. I could simply write three blog posts and say, "There ya go, now you know what those three words mean." That isn't going to make you a better programmer and definitely not a person who can work on their own as a developer for the next 10 or 20 years. Simply knowing *about* process doesn't mean you can actually apply it in real practice. Reading a blog post about creativity doesn't help you find out how *you* are creative with code. To really understand these complex topics you'll want to internalize them, and the best way to do that is to apply them to simple projects.

As you work through the exercises in this book I will tell you which of the three you'll be working on. This is a change from my other books where I try to be sneaky and have you learn concepts without your realization. I'm going to be explicit this time because it's important that you keep the concept firmly in your mind so you can practice it throughout the exercise. You will then evaluate how well your attempt at applying the practice worked and what you can do to improve the next time. A key component of this book is the ability to reflect on your own capabilities objectively and improve yourself. You do this best by being focused on one technique or practice at a time while accomplishing some other goal.

In addition to process, creativity, and quality you'll also learn what I consider six important topics a modern programmer needs to function. These may change in the future, but they've been essential for decades now, so unless there's a drastic shift in technology they'll still apply. Even something like SQL in Part VI is still relevant because it teaches you how to structure data so that it doesn't logically fall apart later. Your secondary educational goals are the following:

1. Getting Started: You learn quick hacks to start a project.

2. Data Structures: I don't teach every single data structure, but I get you started down the path to learning them more completely.

3. Algorithms: Data structures are fairly pointless without a way to process them.

4. Parsing Text: The foundation of computer science is parsing, and knowing how to do that helps you learn programming languages as they become popular.

5. Data Modeling: I use SQL to teach you the basics of modeling stored data in a logical way.

6. Unix Tools: Command line tools are used throughout the book as projects for you to copy, and you then also learn advanced Unix command line tools.

At each part of the book you'll focus on one or two of the three practices at a time until finally, in Part VII, you'll apply them all as you build a simple website. The final projects aren't sexy. You won't learn how to create your next startup, but they are nice little projects that will help you apply what you know while learning Django.

It's All Personal

Many other books are designed to teach you these three concepts in the context of a team. When these books teach you about process it's all about how you work with another person on a project to maintain code. When they teach creativity it's all about how you go to meetings with your team to ask customers questions. Sadly most of these "professional" books don't really teach quality. This is all fine, but there's two problems with these team-style books for most beginners:

1. You don't have a team, so you can't practice what they're teaching. The team-oriented books are designed for junior programmers who already have jobs and need to work on the team they just joined. Until that happens to you, any team-oriented book is fairly useless to you.

2. What's the point of learning how to work on a team if your own personal process, creativity, and quality is a total mess? Despite what the fans of "team players" say, the vast majority of programming tasks are done solo, and your evaluation of your skills is usually done solo. If you work on a team, but your code is always low quality and you constantly have to ask team members for help, you get a low review from your boss. For all their talk of how awesome teams are, they never blame the team when a junior programmer can't work alone. They blame the junior programmer.

This book is *not* about being a good worker drone at Mega Enterprise, LLC. This book is about helping *you* improve *your personal skills* so that when you get a job you can work alone. If you improve your personal process then it makes sense that you'll be a stronger contributor on a team. It also means you can start and develop your own ideas, which is where the vast majority of projects start.

Using the Included Videos

Learn More Python 3 the Hard Way has an extensive set of videos demonstrating how the code works, debugging, and, most importantly, solutions to the challenges. The videos are the perfect place to demonstrate many common errors by breaking the Python code on purpose and showing you how to fix it. I also walk through the code using debugging and interrogation tricks and techniques. The videos are where I show you how to "stop staring and ask" the code what's wrong. You can watch these videos online at informit.com/title/9780134123486.

Register your copy of *Learn More Python 3 the Hard Way* on the InformIT site for convenient access to updates and corrections as they become available. To start the registration process, go to informit.com/register and log in or create an account. Enter the product ISBN (9780134123486) and answer the simple proof-of-purchase question. Then look on the Registered Products tab for an Access Bonus Content link next to this product, and follow that link to access the bonus materials.

PART I
Initial Knowledge

The very first thing you need to learn is everything. I know that's intimidating, but as I mentioned in the preface, you are going to practice only three skills for the entire book. Each exercise is going to enforce each of the skills as you complete other tasks. I may tell you to "make a copy of the `cat` command," but what you are really learning is how to be creative. I may tell you to "create a linked list data structure," but what you're really doing is applying structured code review processes to your programming practice. The secret of this book is that you are only using the projects and exercises as a vehicle to learn three important practices: process, creativity, and quality.

Ideally there's nothing magical about these three concepts. Process is simply the steps you use to create something. Creativity is simply how you generate and implement ideas. Quality is simply how you make sure those implementations aren't junk. The meat is in the application. How *do* you apply a process to your personal development skills? How *do* you analyze whether you've been building quality software or not? How *do* you take an idea and turn it into reality? All three of these are interconnected as you need a process to help you get creative and then a process for ensuring quality, which also requires being creative since no process works all the time. It's a vicious, beautiful cycle.

The process for completing this book is simply this:

1. I will give you a goal of working on process, creativity, or quality for a part of the book. Usually it will be two concepts at a time; sometimes just one. For example, in Part II you are working on creativity by hacking on simple tools in a 45-minute fast session. You are also analyzing your starting process since, if you find it difficult to start, you won't be very creative.

2. The beginning of each exercise will give you a prompt or goal to think about while you work on the exercise. Each of these prompts will ask you to focus on one or more aspects of what you're working on. Exercise 4 in Part II gives you the task of simply implementing something, and then in Exercise 5 you start to list the things that blocked you and try to eliminate them or make them more efficient. Other exercises ask you to look at your physical environment and fix anything distracting. For each exercise you'll think about these prompts and then work on the exercise, attempting to focus on that particular task.

3. At the end of each exercise there are Study Drills that give you more challenges to work on. They might be related to the project or they might be more about the process, creativity, or quality issue you're dealing with in the exercise.

4. Some exercises are in "challenge mode." That means you are given a description of a tool to implement, usually based on an existing Unix tool, and then told to implement it but without any code to look at. There may be small pieces of sample code you'll need to study first, but usually there is no Python in these challenges. The solutions are available online in a Git project at http://bit.ly/lmpthwsolve on Github.

5. Other exercises will be educational descriptions of something you have to implement based on my code. These exercises will explain something, such as an algorithm, and then you are to implement them as exactly as possible and find any bugs you can. Typically these exercises will focus on quality, since you'll be asked to write automated tests, track your error rates, and find solutions to additional problems in the Study Drills.

6. Finally, you'll use a Lab Journal to take notes and keep track of metrics you can use to improve how *you* work. I am very explicit about treating this as a journal, meaning a very private personal account of your improvement that you should not share with anyone—especially nobody who is a manager at your company. This kind of information can be used to take advantage of you as a worker, so guard it carefully.

Your goal when going through this book is not just to whip up a few copies of some Unix tools. Your goal is to *use* these small Unix tool projects to focus on aspects of your ability to work on larger projects.

What If I Hate Your Stupid Personal Process Zed?

That's completely alright. This book is meant to be something that helps you grow and improve, so if you are not quite ready to analyze how you work then save that for later. You can simply do all of the challenges in your own way and your own time, then come back and attempt the projects with the constraints on your process. Every exercise stands on its own and the personal development portions apply to almost anything you work on. Do what you can and come back when you need to work on how you work.

What If I Find Out I'm Terrible?

That is a very real possibility, but my method works to help you know *why* you are terrible and what to do in order to fix it. Then it's just a matter of working on it until you start getting better. Keep your journal private, and nobody will know just how terrible you are. Then when you're done you'll know *exactly* where you stand and what you need to work on. No more guessing at whether you're a fraud or can really do the job. You'll objectively know your strengths and weaknesses so you can stop worrying about where you stand in the world.

However, you probably are not as terrible as you think. This book is meant to be a private course in improving your *objective* outlook on your skills. That means you should be focusing not on how good you are at something, but how much you *improve*. If you find yourself getting upset at your performance on a particular exercise then you need to break it down and find out what you can improve. You also need to look at that one exercise in the context of all the others you've completed and objectively rate your improvement. Focusing on improvement helps you think objectively (not positively or negatively) and keep learning.

The Setup

You are going to need to set up and configure some tools to use this book. Chances are that you may already have many of these, but let's just make sure.

A Programmer's Editor

You need a *programmer's* text editor, not an IDE. Vim, Emacs, and Atom are all programmer's text editors. They're not simplistic text editors that can only do text, but instead are designed for you to manage whole projects and work with lots of programming files at once. They also have common features found in IDEs like running build commands, scripting, and others, but there's one key difference: An IDE is typically tied to one single language because it does advanced introspection on the source and provides you with shortcuts to write the code. You then don't have to remember anything and can just CTRL-Space your way through most any project. This is awesome when you have 100 other 10x developers who are writing more technical debt than you can handle, but it's a terrible feature when you're trying to learn. The other problem is you have to wait around for someone to write you an IDE for any new languages, so if Microsoft or JetBrains don't like a language then you are stuck.

Everything you can do with an IDE you can also do with a real programmer's text editor, and since editors like Vim, Emacs, and Atom are scriptable and modifiable they are future proof. If Haskell++ becomes the next hotness, you can work with it now and all your past projects at the same time. If you become dependant on an IDE, then you've got to wait for someone else to figure out the language for you.

If you are just starting out and want to get a decent programmer's editor that is free, then you should get Atom (https://atom.io) or VisualStudio Code (https://code.visualstudio.com). These editors run on every platform I use in the book, are scriptable, have many plugins, and are easy to use. You can also use Vim or Emacs if you want.

Python 3.6

This book requires Python 3.6. In theory you could use Python 2.7 since many of the exercises are challenges with no code. However, the videos will feature Python 3.6 in the solutions, and the official code repository for solutions will be in Python 3.6 as well. That means you'll have problems translating the solutions back to Python 2.7. If you do not know Python 3.6, then you can read *Learn Python 3 the Hard Way* to get the basics.

A Working Terminal

If you've gone through *Learn Python 3 the Hard Way* then you know that I have you use the Terminal. By now you shouldn't need to be told how to get it started, but, just in case, the set up video shows you several options. This video is useful on Windows since the landscape of Terminal support and shell scripting is changing dramatically at Microsoft, and they're now supporting a much larger and broader range of Unix tooling.

A Working `pip+virtualenv` Configuration

This book requires the installation of a *lot* of additional libraries and software. In the Python world this is most easily done with `pip` and `virtualenv`. The `pip` tool installs packages off the internet and puts them on your computer so you can `import` them in your Python scripts. The problem with `pip` is you are forced to install it in official directories on your computer that require `root` or Administrator access. The solution to this is the tool `virtualenv`, which creates a kind of "python package sandbox" in a directory and then allows you to run `pip` to install packages there rather than into the whole main computer. In the setup video I'll show you how to install and make sure you have `pip+virtualenv` for all the platforms and use it.

Lab Journal

You are going to be taking notes and recording metrics while you research projects. You'll want to get a book of graph paper or possibly paper with dots rather than lines for graphs and a good bag of pencils. You can use whatever you like, but part of the process used in this book is to keep track of things outside the computer as a way of changing your viewpoint while you solve problems. It's also possible that you've been using paper longer than a computer (although, that may be changing), so you may feel that paper is more "real" and the computer just doesn't make sense. Writing things on paper first and then translating them into the computer will help you get past this perceptual difficulty. Finally, drawing on paper is just easier.

A Github.com Account

You will want to go to github.com and sign up for an account if you don't already have one. I will be giving you free code for all of the video presentations and all of the projects so you can check your work. If you get stuck you can check out the project for this book and take a peak at how I solved it. There will also be times when I tell you to go fix a project that I have purposefully left buggy as an exercise.

git

If you have a github.com account then you'll also need the command line tool `git`. github.com will have plenty of information on how and where to get it, but watch the setup video to see how best to install it for your platform.

Optional: Screen-Recording Software

This isn't required, but if you can get software to record your screen, and ideally your face at the same time, then this will help you analyze how you work. I say this is optional because it could be a little too much to have full recordings of your work that you then go over and pick apart for clues about how to improve your process. I did it for a while, and it helped me so much, but it also kind of killed my creativity. My recommendation is that if you can afford or find screen recording software, then you should use it when you feel that you simply can't figure out what you are doing wrong and need to watch yourself work. I also think recording your actual face and body while you work is helpful to check whether you have bad posture or other physical habits that may be causing you physical pain, but again, recording yourself all day while you work is a bit too much. It's also something you can't really do at a job with other people.

Further Study

That is all of the things you need right now. As the book continues I'll be instructing you on other things you need at specific times. To finish this exercise you should now watch the video for your platform and then install all the things I tell you to. If you have something already installed, then the video has things to do that confirm your gear is in working order. Watch it to make sure you can follow along with the rest of the book.

On Process

There are two types of processes in the world of software development. First you have the Team Process, which encompasses things like Scrum, Agile, and eXtreme Programming (XP). These processes are designed to help a team of people coordinate around a large codebase without killing each other. A Team Process is one that dictates how each person will coordinate, standards of code behavior, reporting, and management oversight. Usually these Team Processes boil down to:

1. Make a list of things to do.

2. Do the things on the list.

3. Confirm they are done correctly.

Where many Team Processes go wrong is when they try to control personal processes that are better left to an individual. The XP process is probably the most abusive in this respect, going so far as to dictate that each programmer have another programmer who observes their work and yells at them whenever the text editor shows some red. I strongly object to processes that force personal process elements onto people when not in some educational context. It insults our professionalism and creates an environment of dictatorial condescension that does not foster creativity or quality. In an educational setting, dictating that students use particular personal process methods is necessary but not in the work environment. For example, the only time I *force* paired programming on someone is if they are a junior programmer or new to the team and need to learn. After that the team process should be such that everyone is able to work however they need to get the job done at the required quality level.

The other type of process is a Personal Process, and I take this idea from painters, writers, and musicians. Part of developing as a creative individual who focuses on quality is developing a process that helps you produce work in a consistent way. In fact, a sign of an amateur painter, musician, or writer is one who has no idea about their process. Usually these people who claim to have no creative process actually do have one; they just aren't aware of it and therefore constantly get it wrong. Most other creative disciplines develop strategies and tactics that help them create finished works from ideas without falling into disaster half-way through. For painters this is a way of breaking the problem of a painting down into logical steps that assure success is more likely. With musicians it's a similar process combined with a balancing act of staying within the structure of their chosen musical style. With writers their process is a way to structure their writing so that it flows naturally and isn't full of plot holes and logical inconsistencies (something most TV writers seem to totally not get).

For software your Personal Process needs to be something that accomplishes the following:

1. Identifies viable ideas to work on

2. Gets you started on those ideas to see if they'll work and changes them quickly

3. Progressively refines your ideas over numerous work sessions in a way that avoids problems or enables you to recover easily

4.   Ensures the quality of your implementation of your ideas so that you aren't crushed by the weight of bugs later

5.   Makes sure you can work with others (if you want)

Notice how I say you don't *have* to work with others. Since the advent of open source the concept of creating software has included an overbearing demand for community. If you don't want to share or work with others, then you are an insult to their being and considered an antisocial cowboy. The problem is very few creative activities are started in a group, and usually the ones that are started in a group end up not being creative at all. That creative spark is usually the result of one or maybe two people having an idea and then realizing it from nothing. Producing a finished product can require a large team, as with books, movies, and albums. Many other creative activities can be done solo, such as with painting or most visual arts.

You'll never find an art school demanding that painters only work in teams to create a painting. There's also no reason that software can't be a solo creative process similar to painting and writing. Software is a modular discipline, which means you can create something all by yourself and other people can still use it even if they never talk to you and never work on it. You can be a total jerk and people can still use your software. Writing and painting are the same way. There's an ocean of miscreant, abusive writers, painters, and musicians who are still worshiped by millions of people.

If you start working on your personal process and someone tries to tell you that you need to share or you're an antisocial jerk, then they're being abusive. People have the right to keep things private, work alone, and make their own things. The only people who seem to demand that you contribute to larger projects are the people who started those larger projects and seem to make all the money. Trust me on this. I've contributed a huge amount to the world of software, and still I go to conferences and people say I'm not a contributor because I didn't write lines of code into their project (even though they've never ever done a single thing to help me).

Throughout this book, when I say "process" I mean *personal* process. I rarely cover anything that directly relates to working with others because there's a mountain of books that already cover how you should work with others. There's very few books that help you work on your own process and define what works for you and why. There's absolutely nothing wrong, self-centered, greedy, antisocial, or abusive about wanting to focus on you so you can be better at what you love.

Exercise Challenge

The actual exercise is to just write down what you think your process is and what problems you seem to have. At this stage you might have no idea how you work because you aren't very experienced. To help you I've compiled a list of questions:

* Do you have problems working on projects for long periods of time?

* Do you tend to make defective code with no idea why?

* Do you chase programming languages but never actually implement anything?

- Do you never remember APIs? (Yeah, me neither.)

- Do you feel inferior or like a fraud who will get caught?

- Do you worry whether you're a "real programmer"?

- Do you have no idea how to take an idea and pop it out of your head into code?

- Do you have problems getting started?

- Do you work in a chaotic environment?

- Do you get past the first implementation of your project and have no idea how to take it further?

- Do you keep piling code on top of code until there's just a huge mess?

Think about these questions, then try to write down what you do when you work on a project. If you don't have experience working on something, then write down what you *think* you should do on a project.

Study Drills

1. Write some more questions like this, then answer them.

2. Ask other programmers you may know what their process is. You'll find they probably have no idea.

Further Study

Something to keep in mind is that what people *say* their process is and what they actually do can be wildly different. We humans have a tendency to remember events in a much more positive, logical way than reality. During this book you're going to break this habit and use externally recorded metrics (and possibly screen recording) to know for *sure* what you do. This isn't something you should do forever, but it's a big help when you're working on improving your coding skills. But, when you ask some other more successful programmer what their process is just keep in mind that they have not done this and most likely what they tell you is not really what they do. If you can find a more experienced programmer willing to record their screen while they work, then that can be more instructive than asking them what they do. I suggest going to the screencasts of other programmers and simply watching how they tackle problems and taking notes.

On Creativity

C reativity is nothing special. If you're a person of average or more intelligence, then you are creative. Being able to have thoughts and ideas which you then turn into reality is simply an aspect of human intelligence and thought. The problem is creativity has become a calling card for a special magical class of person called The Creative. There are entire books describing this mythical priest of the art world who can imagine an idea, and with a wave of their insanely creative golden hands, craft pure emotionally intelligent empathic works of art that make the babies of heaven weep tears of pure platinum. Frankly the word "creativity" is an overused cliché that is used to segregate people from implementing their ideas, but I have no choice but to use that word in this book.

In my book the word "creativity" only means "forming an idea into the real world." I do not imply any superiority with the word, nor any magical significance to people who are adept at realizing thoughts. The only difference between me—a supposedly very creative person—and you is that I've practiced taking ideas I have and making them real. I keep a notebook of ideas and try to implement them regularly. I study painting, music, writing, and programming as a means of implementing and crafting my thoughts into realities. By simply attempting to create something on a regular basis I've become adept at doing it, and there is no magic to this. I just keep trying until I can do it.

The process of learning to create what I have in my mind has produced an epic number of mountainous piles of junk, but at the tops of those piles of junk are some works I admire. If you want to work on your ability to create, then you too will have to make your own junk piles. But you can't just randomly create a pile of junk and hope to be awesome when you reach the top. The trick to being a *productive* creative person is learning to implement your ideas inside a process or set of constraints that guides you on a path of learning but avoiding the trap of a strict process that kills your creativity. The balancing act of an imaginative person is on the line between a process that guides you and the process that kills your ideas. It's my hope that in this book you'll find that sweet spot.

Exercise Challenge

To work on your creative process you'll first need to work on being random. I think one of my main strengths is the ability to take two seemingly random ideas and turn them into something interesting or useful. You can start working on this by doing this little exercise every day:

1. Write down at least three randomly combined words. Idiotic forests have iguanas. Symbolism begets crepes. Python could summon aliens.

2. Then spend 10 minutes writing an essay about these three words, or one of them, that goes through as many of your senses as you can imagine—sight, sound, sense of balance, taste, smell. Look up how many different senses humans actually have to get an idea of what you

can write. Don't censor yourself, just let the words flow. You can also draw the idea, paint, or write poetry.

3. During this exercise you might suddenly have actual ideas related to software or other topics of interest. Write these down in a more serious location for later exploration, or even draw them if you can.

Believe it or not, this one simple little exercise will improve a great many things when you sit down to implement software:

1. It teaches you to let your ideas flow and not censor them.

2. It trains you to freely associate seemingly disconnected ideas to find possible connections.

3. It opens your mind to possibility without self-criticism.

4. It improves your ability to articulate your thoughts in writing or drawing, which is usually a first step in turning ideas into reality.

5. It forces you to imagine how your senses might work and also how they work for other people, which helps you implement them in the real world.

6. It also tricks people into thinking you're super deep and an Artiste. You might as well go buy yourself a beret and move to Paris after this.

This process of randomly writing and thinking about absurd concepts can be tough for people who are used to sweating the details of software and worrying about quality. That's completely understandable, and you definitely *still* need that sense of quality you've developed. Creativity without a sense of critical quality only produces junk. However, quality without creativity lacks the imagination necessary to see what might go wrong with something you've created. What you need is that mixture of both creativity and quality that helps you create software and make sure it's solid.

Study Drill

If you don't like the idea of writing down random words like, "Unitarians tend to fly omelets," then you can simply pick a random word from a dictionary and write about that from your senses. This works just as well and also doesn't feel frivolous, but I'll encourage you to be a little frivolous. Nobody ever got fired for writing poetry about gold-coated bees on the coast of pearls. Another option is to express how you feel from the point of view of all your senses. This can also help you be creative and is rather therapeutic too.

On Quality

I 'm going to propose a scientific theory about cognition I cannot prove:

The act of remembering what you did makes you think the end product is correct.

This is from an observation in nearly every creative thing I've ever done that goes something like this:

1. You create something requiring a long period of time. This could be software, a painting, writing, or anything that takes time.

2. You "finish" and then step back to marvel at how good it is, when a friend walks up.

3. Your friend then points out one glaringly obvious problem, and suddenly your entire vision of what you created changes.

4. Now all you see is this mistake your friend pointed out, and you have no idea how you possibly missed it.

I believe that this phenomenon happens because you have memories of how you made it that are influencing your concept of what you perceive. The act of creating tends to be a positive flow of ideas and work, so your memories are more on the positive or neutral side. This then colors your perception of the work to make you think it's way more awesome than it really is but also hides many flaws and details. There is also an emotional attachment to the work since you created it and remember doing it, which clouds your judgment of the work. Your friend, however, has none of these memories and sees the work more objectively, which makes it easier to see the flaws. This is why copy editors find many more errors than writers. Or, why security professionals find many more defects in software than those who created the software. These external reviewers simply have no emotional attachment and no memories of how you created it, so they see it more clearly.

In the world of painting this is so common that painters have numerous tricks to subvert the phenomenon. These tricks are even mentioned by Leonardo da Vinci in his notebooks, and they're designed to give the painter the perspective of their critical friend:

- Turn the painting upside down and look at it from farther away. This points out obvious problems with color and contrast while also showing you repeating shapes you need to alter. In fine art repetitive shapes are undesirable.

- Look at the painting in a mirror, which flips it horizontally so your brain has no concept of how it was created. Flipping it horizontally turns it into a fresh new painting you've never seen before, and then suddenly you are the obnoxious critical friend.

- Look at the painting through a red glass or in a black mirror, which removes color and only shows it in black and white. This shows areas where the painting is too bright or dark, which makes it look strange in color.

- Look at both the painting and subject through a mirror placed on their forehead, looking up into the mirror, which flips both the painting and the subject upside down so you can compare the two. This shows obvious problems with drawing and makes both the scene and painting look like abstract shapes your brain has no memory of.

- Put the painting away for a few months so you forget how you did it then take it out to look again.

- Ask your obnoxious friend to look at it and have them tell you what they see.

Some painters go so far as to have a mirror behind them while they paint so they can simply turn around to check their progress. I frequently use a black mirror (or just my mobile phone's screen when it's turned off) placed on my forehead to check paintings.

In other creative disciplines there are not as many of these self-criticism techniques, and in software there are very few. In fact, I find that programmers are notorious for being "programmer done" with their code. "Programmer done" is where a programmer hacks and hacks on a piece of code, piling it on until it barely compiles, then declares their work done and moves on. The truth is there's a mountain of work to do after that, from cleaning the code up, performing quality assurance checks, adding invariants and assertions, writing tests, writing documentation, and confirming it works within the larger context of the whole system. But nope, programmers are frequently done when the compiler (or test suite) runs without errors.

In this book you're going to learn to conduct your *own* set of checks that are similar to what painters use. They are ways of looking at your code disconnected from the history of how you made it, and the secret is going to be checklists. The way you subvert your memories of your work is to force yourself to follow a set of checks that assume you've written something defective. The quality process I'm teaching you won't catch everything, but it will help you spot as many errors as you can find yourself and also help you track what kinds of errors you keep making so you can avoid them in the future. After that you'll be encouraged to have *other* people audit your code and also audit other people's code so you can get fresh eyes to find even more flaws.

The philosophy I have with defect reduction is one of probabilities. You cannot remove all defects, ever. Instead you'll work on reducing the probability that there is a defect and be able to give a rough estimate of that chance. This frees you from the panic of not knowing if your code is defective and helps you get an idea of how you keep making bad software. Instead of being "programmer done" all the time, you'll have a good idea of when you are finished and ready for review. Instead of being constantly worried about every impossible edge case, you'll be able to assess the probability of these edge cases and deal with the most likely ones.

Exercise Challenge

In this exercise you are going to find a piece of code you wrote months ago and then review it. You may not know how to audit a piece of code yet, but just go through and write comments in the code for anything you find that you do not like. The key is to go line by line and file by file and look at each line of code. You will then tag that code you find objectionable and write out why. It doesn't have to be a very large piece of software, just something you wrote a while ago.

Study Drill

Compile a list of all the defects you found doing this and try categorize them. You can look up official defect categories, but a good basic set is logic, data type, and calling. A logic error is when you write an if-statement or loop that's wrong. A data type error is when you used a variable and assumed it was the wrong type. A calling error is when you called a function and did it wrong. These aren't official categories, but they're a good start for you at this time.

PART II
Quick Hacks

You've got the best idea ever. You're going to impress the world! You'll be a billionaire! Your brain is enflamed with the concept and you see it in your dreams haunting you like a Yurei. The next step is to make it real, to implement it and bring it out of your brain and into the computer. You have to kill the ghost, bring the Yurei back from the spirit world and bind it to a totem of Python and sticks that you throw into the sea of the internet.

Creative enough for you?

The enemy of creativity is the start. How can you realize your dreams if there's an obstacle course of setup procedures and dead yaks in the way? What if your idea is so intense and so big that you begin to worry? Will you be good enough? Will you be smart enough? Will that famous programmer who always yells at you to write your tests first be angry that you don't know how to do it? Getting started is universally one of the most difficult things in creativity, and this part of the book is designed to get you past that.

I am a painter, a musician, a writer, and a programmer, so I know a thing or two about creativity. I know even more about getting started and about process. Process is what drags me through the muddy slog of a project when I'm just *not* interested in working on it anymore. But, I can't get to that slog without first getting started.

The start requires courage and a bit of not caring what anyone thinks. In painting, when I can't get started I just grab any random paint and smack it on the canvas in about the right spot. A whole lot of very accomplished painters work that way. Other painters get through the start by doing research—studying, testing, sketching, and then finally pulling it all together to begin. As a writer, the first thing I do is walk around my apartment frantically talking to myself imagining I'm talking to someone, and then when I've done enough talking I sit down and write. I just write down the first things that come to mind.

I don't sit down to write and worry about grammar. I don't ask, "Do I sound smart?" I just write how I speak and flow it into the keyboard, and then when I'm done cranking out a few paragraphs I take a look. Does it make sense? Do I need to clean up? It works and this gets me flowing and going. Maybe what I write is total garbage. But, I started and that's what's important then. After this I rely on my process to turn the starting point into a fully baked word.

How do *you* learn your creative start? You, my friend, need to figure that out, and this book will help. First we need to bust your fear of the start. Maybe it's not even fear. Maybe you just have a metric ton of totally useless tasks you need to do before you begin coding and you've *got* to get the friction out of your way.

How to Practice Creativity

In this part of the book you will practice creativity by making yourself start right away and quickly. I'll give you simple little projects that are super boring. I mean, the `cat` command from Unix just spews out a file. That's honestly like two lines of Python as the simplest case. It's the start of these projects that matter, and you're going to be ruthless about getting going. You're going to sit down at your computer and jump off a cliff and make things happen. Now. Not after 30 minutes.

How do you do this? You need a checklist, and you need automation. The checklist is all the things you have to do to get ready to go. Turn on your computer, turn off social media, fire up your editor, touch your lucky rubber ducky, say a prayer to a deity, meditate for 10 minutes, and then copy your project skeleton over and go. That's an example, but you'll need a check list, and the shorter that checklist the better.

But you don't know what this checklist is yet. Maybe you have an idea, but do you *really* know all the things you do before you start working? That's what you'll focus on with each of these projects. In the first project, you'll sit down to attempt it, but you'll *write down all the things you did*. You can't manage what you can't measure, and this is your first step into measuring yourself to see how you do something. If you have screen recording software that would be *even better*. Turn that on and record yourself cranking out a terrible piece of software, then watch the video. Write down what you did.

To make sure you don't slave away at the project rather than practice the start you're also going to set a strict timer on each project. You have to crank out the best piece of junk you can in 45 minutes. No more, no less. Set a 45 minute timer when you start, have your pad and pencil ready, and go. When the timer goes off you're done. Take a look at what you did, and then comes the good part.

After each project take your list and figure out what you can do to *eliminate the friction*. Do you sit there and make many little files that you have to look up on the internet? Make a project skeleton. Do you seem to have a problem typing commands at your text editor? Spend the time to learn to use it better, or learn to touch type. Do you flap around, not knowing basic commands and APIs? Get some books and study, my friend.

Then *erase* your code and start over. Fresh. New pad of paper and begin to write. Or start recording. Whatever you have to do to track what you do. Did you get farther this time? Was there less friction? Your goal is to reduce the time between idea and implementation until the start is just a thing you do. Like eating and breathing. Eventually the start will feel natural and you can move on to the next project.

Remember that you are to sit down and code right away. Just go. If an internal voice tells you that you're doing it wrong, tell that stupid voice to shut its pedantic mouth. This is hacking. Keep it loose and pump it out like you're just blabbing the code out to a friend who knows you're kind of nuts but still fun. Pedantic things like testing and quality can come later in the book, but for now, just code. Make a mess and hack. It's fun. Getting the idea out is more important than winning an imaginary quality contest.

And after each sloppy 45-minute hack, sit down and review how you did. This process of "create then critique" is what's going to help you improve in the future.

A Process for Early Coders

If you are just starting out and still completely lost when it comes to starting a project then I'm going to give you an abbreviated process to use to get you started. The exercise in this part is to hack for 45 minutes, but as an early programmer you may need a little more time or you may not know where to start. In this case, feel free to take 60 minutes or to use two 45 minute sessions to do each exercise.

For a process, an early programmer should do the following before every session (before you start the timer):

1. Get your computer ready and make sure you are ready to go.

2. Read the description of the task and write down notes. This is your research phase and you need to gather as much information as you can in written form.

3. Take your research and turn it into a TODO list of what you need to do to implement the hack. Write down everything you can think of for the task. What files will you need to make? What directories? What features? What libraries will you use?

Once you have the TODO list you are ready to start the timer. During your hacking session you will then do this:

1. Pick the first simplest task on your TODO and do it. Do you need a file? Make it! Do you need a directory? Make it!

2. Check that what you just did works.

3. Cross that task off and do the next one.

I am serious about this process. It's a smaller version of the one I use and it works. Nearly every process is simply "make a list, do it, check it." If it works for me it will work for you, so you should use it if you have no idea what to do.

An Early Coder's Coding Process

This process will also work for the code you write. I covered this in *Learn Python 3 the Hard Way*. When you are unsure how to write a piece of code follow this process:

1. Write in plain English what your code should do. If you need to write it as a paragraph, then do it. If you can write it as a list of tasks, that's better. If you write a paragraph you'll then convert that to a list of things the code must do.

2. Turn this list into comments by putting # in front of each line.

3. Start at the top, and under each comment, write the Python code that makes it work. If the comment is too abstract then break it up into smaller comments and repeat this step.

4. Run the code to make sure what you just wrote doesn't have syntax errors and will mostly work.

That's all you need to do. If you can say what you want the code to do in English (or any human language) then you'll be able to implement it easily and don't have to think in code. Eventually you won't need to write comments first and fill in the code, but when I'm stuck I still do this.

Dealing with Command Line Arguments

B efore you can work on this part of the book you need to do some quick hacking that teaches you about command line arguments in Python.

Traditionally we call this kind of hacking a "spike." The term comes from doing a small test project that covers all of the elements of a larger process or project. This little test hack "spikes" through everything to make sure you can use it. The purpose of a spike is to figure out how to use some new library or tool in a dress rehearsal before you sit down to really use it in your project.

This is also the first exercise in challenge mode. Challenge mode is designed to make *you* figure out how to do something, and then you can come and see how I did it compared to your work. I don't give you the code first and have you type it in. Nope, that's for beginners and you're no longer a beginner. You are now reading a challenge and then you have to solve it.

WARNING! Read this very carefully! You are not expected to complete a fully working publishable piece of software in 45 minutes. The 45-minute time limit is to make you get going and stop worrying that you'll do it wrong. It's a push to make you work and *not* intended as a test. This means that if you look at the 45-minute time frame and then freeze because you think you can't get a monumental piece of beauty completed you are *doing this wrong*. You should look at this as, "Let's see what I can get done in 45 minutes." These exercises are open ended because different people will complete different amounts of work in the given time. You are simply using the time constraint to figure out how you work, not to figure out if you are a terrible programmer or a great one.

Exercise Challenge

You are to write two tiny Python scripts that test out processing command line arguments using two methods:

1.   Plain old `sys.argv` like you would do normally.

2.   Python's `argparse` package, for more fancy argument handling.

Your test script should be able to handle the following situations:

1.   Getting help with `—help` or `-h`.

2.   At least three arguments that are flags, meaning they don't take an extra argument but simply putting them on the command line turns something on.

3. At least three arguments that are options, meaning they do take an argument and set a variable in your script to that option.

4. Additional "positional" arguments, which are lists of files at the end of all the – style arguments and can handle Terminal wildcards like `*/.txt`.

Since this exercise is a spike you should have the attitude that if something is a pain during your test you can abandon it and try the other thing. Start with trying to solve this with `sys.argv`, and then if you just can't figure it out try `argparse` instead.

Remember that this is a timed *45-minute* exercise and you need to stick to that. You must also keep track of everything you do to get started. Your purpose with this exercise is to figure out how *you* keep getting in your own way to start a project. Are you talking yourself out of it before you even start? Do you not know where your text editor is or how to use it? Write it down, and then figure out how to remove that friction.

However, do not confuse this strict 45-minute exercise with failure. You are attempting to do something, anything, in 45 minutes. If your skill level is such that you get an `ex4.py` file written and nothing else then you did *something* in 45 minutes. You should then take a look at why all you did was start that file, figure out what you need to do next time, and then attempt another 45-minute session.

Solution

To keep you from cheating, the code to all of the solutions is in the book's project site at http://bit.ly/lmpthwsolve, which is hosted on github.com. Rather than include the code here so you are tempted to cheat and just take a little peek at it, you'll have to go check out the project and navigate to the ex4 directory to see how I did this hack. You'll also find my notes on how I did my start and what I could improve.

WARNING! Remember, if you get stuck to refer back to the introduction to Part II and use the Process for Early Coders I gave you. You make a list, do the list, check what you did. That's it.

Study Drills

1. How many other Python argument parsing libraries are there? Is there one you like better?

2. What's the main advantage of `argparse` over `sys.argv`?

3. What are things you can improve in your project starting method? Is there something you can eliminate now?

cat

With Exercise 4 you began the work of finding out what blocks you. It was a simple challenge of conducting a spike researching how best to get command line arguments from a user. The real purpose of the exercise was your lab notes on what *you* do to get started. Did you discover anything you need to change? Any strange habits or setup issues? In this exercise you'll be creating a replica of a simple command called `cat`, but your real purpose is to pick one thing to change about your setup so you get started faster. Remember that the point is *not* your implementation of `cat`. The point is how quickly can you get started and whether you can do something useful in 45 minutes.

As with the previous exercise, stick to the 45-minute deadline. Setting limits on how much time you'll spend on an exercise is a useful technique to get you into the mode of coding. In fact, if you can warm up with a 45-minute hack every day that would be an *ideal* practice going forward. Before you can do that you'll need to get better at starting, so figure out what friction you're going to kill today and let's begin.

WARNING! I will state this one more time so that it is clear: You cannot fail at this exercise. If you approach the 45-minute limit as a graded exercise and set any expectations for how well you should or should not do then you are doing this wrong. The correct way to think about the 45 minutes is simply as a device to kick you in the rear and get you going. It is not a test. I repeat, it is not a test. Keep telling yourself that so you relax and just go for it.

Exercise Challenge

The `cat` command is short for "concatenate," and it's most commonly used to dump the contents of a file to the screen. You use it like this:

```
cat somefile.txt
```

This command will spit out the contents of `somefile.txt`. That's not actually its original purpose. Originally it was for combining more than one file—thus it was called `cat`. To do that simply add each file to `cat`:

```
cat A.txt B.txt C.txt
```

The `cat` command will then go through each file, write its contents out, and then exit when it has gone through all of them. The problem is, how does this possibly concatenate files? To do that you'll also need to use the POSIX file redirection features found in your Terminal:

```
cat A.txt B.txt C.txt > D.txt
```

The use of the > symbol should be familiar to you, and if not then you need to refresh yourself on basic Unix shell operation. It simply takes the standard output of the cat command (which in this case is the contents of A.txt, B.txt, and C.txt all combined) and writes it to the file on the right D.txt.

You are to reimplement as much of the cat command as quickly as you can, using what you learned from Exercise 4 to get command line arguments. Remember that to do standard output you just use print in Python. To learn more about cat use the man system like this:

```
man cat
```

That is the manual for the cat command, and you get bonus points for implementing as much of it as you can in the 45-minute time slot.

Solution

You can find my solution to the problem at the project repository at http://bit.ly/lmpthwsolve on GitHub. It will be in ex5/, and you'll see I did a fairly quick and dirty solution. If you began this exercise worried about quality or creativity then you are doing this wrong. Your job is to be sloppy, be fast, and *get it done*. The point of the time limit is to get you past this notion that every time you touch the keyboard you have to produce a golden code calf to worship. Do it as best you can, and then *afterward* you can go analyze and see what to improve.

Study Drills

1. Were there any surprising features of cat that you have never used or were difficult to implement?

2. Were you able to remove your one friction blocker from your starting process? This is more important than implementing cat, so if you didn't avoid that blocker then you need to do this exercise again.

3. Did you identify more things that are getting in your way? Simple things like your neck hurts because where you sit is too low? Not being a good touch typer? How about your mental state? Were there things you thought that blocked you? Can you stop thinking them?

Further Study

This isn't a self-help book, and I'm not going to fix your psychology, but I find that a huge blocker to learning something new isn't the subject but rather your fears. If in this exercise you found that damaging thoughts or fears were keeping you from getting started, then I suggest you start doing 10 minutes of journaling about how you feel *before* you do your 45-minute hack. Writing down your fears, anxieties, and feelings will articulate them and helps you see how impractical it is to worry about them for something as tiny as a 45 minute hack. Try it. You'd be surprised what 10 minutes of writing about your feelings does for your feelings.

find

Hopefully you are discovering the various ways you sabotage yourself even before you begin to work. Maybe it's not that dramatic, but you should at least be identifying things you can improve in your environment that are making it difficult for you to start working. These little exercises are a good way for you to focus on the beginning since they are not that important and fit into a time scale that you can analyze. If these projects were hours long, you'd get bored reviewing what you've done and making improvements. A short 45-minute project is something you can take notes about (or record) and review very quickly.

This is a pattern I use throughout my studies. I'll identify something that I need to improve on, such as how I get started, or how I handle a tool. Then I'll devise an exercise that simply focuses on that. When I was learning to paint I struggled with going outside to paint trees. I sat down and looked at the problems, and the first thing I identified was I simply dragged too much stuff with me. I also kept all my things in random places around my apartment. I purchased a specific bag just for my painting supplies and kept that bag ready to go. When I wanted to paint outside I grabbed this bag and walked to one of a few places, rather than planning elaborate painting hikes. I practiced just grabbing my bag, walking to one of two places, setting up, doing a painting, then walking home until the process was smooth as silk. After that I watched Bob Ross to figure out how to paint trees because that guy can crank out some trees.

This is what you should be doing. One place many people waste time and effort is in their work area. Do you have a dedicated place to work that never changes? I ditched my laptop and now just use a desktop machine so that I can have a consistent place to do my work. This also saved my back and neck from hauling around that chunk of metal and gave me a bigger screen to work with, all improving my ability to work. In this exercise, I want you to focus on your work area and make sure that it's ready to go before you begin:

1. Do you have enough light? Do you need less light?

2. How's your chair? Do you need a better keyboard?

3. What other tools are getting in the way? Are you trying to do Unix-like things on a Windows machine? Trying to do Mac things on Linux? Don't go buy a new computer, but consider it for your next big purchase if you find there's just too much friction for what you want to do.

4. How's your desk? Do you even have one? Do you hack in cafés all day with terrible chairs and too much coffee?

5. How about music? Do you listen to music with words? I find that if I listen to music without words it's easier for me to focus on the voice in my head that helps me write or code.

6. Do you work in an open plan office and your coworkers are annoying? Go buy yourself a pair of big over-the-ear headphones. When you wear them it's obvious you're not paying attention,

so people will leave you alone and they'll feel it's less rude than if you're plugged in and they can't see. This will also block out distractions and help you focus.

Spend this exercise thinking about topics like this and trying to simplify and enhance your environment. One thing, though: Don't go buying crazy contraptions and spending tons of money. Just identify problems, and then try to find ways to fix them.

Exercise Challenge

In this challenge you are implementing a basic version of the find tool for finding files. You run find like this:

```
find . —name "*.txt" —print
```

That will search the current directory for every file ending in .txt and print it out. find has an insane number of command line arguments, so you are not expected to implement them all in one 45-minute session. The general format of find is the following:

1.　The directory to start searching in: . or /usr/local/

2.　A filter argument like -name or -type d (files of type directory)

3.　An action to do with each found file: -print

You can do useful things like execute a command on every found file. If you want to delete every Ruby file in your home directory you can do this:

```
find . —name "*.rb" —exec rm {} \;
```

Please don't run this without realizing it will delete all the files that end in .rb. The -exec argument takes a command, replaces any instance of {} with the name of the file, and then stops reading the command when it hits a ; (semicolon). We use \; in the preceding command because bash and many other shells use ; as part of their language, so we have to escape it.

This exercise will really test your ability to use either argparse or sys.argv. I recommend you run man find to get a list of arguments, and then try using find to figure out exactly what arguments you'll implement. You only have 45 minutes, so you probably can't get too many, but -name and -type are both essential as well as -print and -exec. The -exec argument will be a challenge though, so save it for last.

When you implement this, try to find libraries that can do the work for you. You'll definitely want to look at the subprocess module and also the glob module. You will definitely want to look at os more carefully as well.

Study Drills

1. How much of `find` did you get implemented?

2. What are the libraries you found to improve this implementation?

3. Did you count finding libraries as part of your 45 minutes? You could say that research before you start hacking doesn't count, and I'd be alright with that. If you want the extra challenge, then include your research in the 45 minutes.

Further Study

How much of `find` can you implement in more 45 minute hacks? Maybe make this your hacking warmup challenge for the next week to see what you can get done. Remember that you should be trying to slap together the best ugly hack you can. Don't worry, I won't tell the Agile people you are just having fun.

grep

The `find` command should have been possible but a good challenge for 45 minutes. At this point you should be knocking down as many blockers to your start as you possibly can imagine. You may find that when you eliminate something your skill gets worse. For example, I used to walk to get a coffee before I started to work. This took me about 30 minutes and was very nice, but that's 30 minutes that many times turned into a few hours. I decided to stop doing that, but then my work suffered. Turns out I still needed coffee, so I bought a nice espresso machine and learned how to make my own lattes. Now I get up and make myself a latte and go do a bit of drawing, which gets me in the mode for doing creative work.

Not everything you do is an innefficiency, so be careful not to eliminate something simply because it takes up time. There are little rituals and personal habits that can get your brain ready to work. The trick is to not eliminate those but to instead make them easier to do before you start working.

You should also be getting a concept of time management during this first part of the book. Setting a time limit of 45 minutes will make it very clear that you have no idea how long you take to do something. With only 45 minutes you can't waste 30 getting your `vim` windows just right and organizing the perfect directory structure then crafting a brand new algorithm for sorting. You have to be frugal in what you implement and in what order you do the work.

A good way to tackle a project is to start with the simplest thing you can get up and running first. In the `find` example that was probably getting a file by a `glob` pattern. Someone with poor time management skills will immediately try to get the `-exec` argument working to prove they are an awesome coder, but `-exec` can't work without `-name` and is much more difficult to implement. The way to decide is to tell yourself that you want something you can *use* when you're done. If 45 minutes passes and you can use `-exec` but can't get files into it then how can you use it? If the same time passes and you've got a way to list files matching a name then you've done it. You have something in 45 minutes.

Keep working your list of blockers and evaluating how well you do with your start, but now start looking at time management. Strategize what you are going to implement so that if you ran out of time you'd have something you can use. They don't have to be complete features, but two useable features is better than 10 that don't work at all because you forgot the simplest thing they all need. Or worse, 10 that don't work because you bounced around half-implementing all of them so none of them work.

Exercise Challenge

You are now going to implement the `grep` command. As usual you should go read `man grep` and then play with it. The purpose of `grep` is to search for text patterns in files using regular expressions. You implemented `find` using the `glob` module, and the operation is similar but done inside a file rather than inside a directory. For example, if I want to search for the word "help" in my book I do this:

```
grep help *.rst
```

The command line arguments to `grep` are fairly simple. The difficult part is handling regular expressions, so you should rely on the `re` module. This module will enable you to load the contents of a file and then search through it for patterns people give you on the command line. Another hint is you will most likely want to load the whole file using `readlines` rather than using `read`. Most of the options to `grep` work better that way even though it is less efficient.

You may also want to briefly skip ahead to Exercise 31 where I give an introduction to regular expressions.

Study Drills

1. Are there special options to the `re` module that make it work more like `grep`?
2. Could you turn your `grep` hack into a module that you then use in your `find` tool to add a `grep` feature?

Further Study

The `re` module is very important, so take the time to really study it and learn everything you can about it. We'll be using it and regular expressions in another part of the book.

cut

Hopefully you're learning more Python but even more about yourself and how you work. In this part of the book you're learning something about process as well as creativity by learning how to refine your process. It's true that you can't be creative with starting friction, but you should also be realizing that the easiest way to improve your own personal process is by watching yourself work. Simply doing exercises isn't enough. You need to take a look at your personal way of working and try to improve on how you do it.

As you refine your starting process you may find that you'll need a couple different starting methods to work on different kinds of projects. When I work on software similar to these little command line tools, I can start with just hacking on the code. When I need to work on anything with a GUI I find that I need to draw the UI out, implement a fake version of it, and then make that work. As you continue with the book you'll learn both ways of working and practice those processes.

In this exercise I want you to focus on your physical health and behavior. Too often programmers wreck their bodies trying to do this job. The job feels like it should not cause you any harm. You're just sitting at a desk all day, not cutting down trees or chasing after criminals in an urban setting. The truth is any job where you sit for long periods of time doing something stressful can destroy your body. To combat that, you're going to keep track of the following things while you work:

1. Do you sit up with good posture? Straight up isn't really good posture, but neither is hunched over. You want to have your body up and relaxed, head held up.

2. Do you pull your shoulders up into your ears? Try to drop them down.

3. Do you tense your wrist and rest them on the desk? Try to float them above the keyboard and keep them not too loose and not too tight.

4. Is your head straight ahead and relaxed or are you straining it to one side to look at another monitor?

5. Is your chair comfortable?

6. Do you take breaks? 45 minutes is the longest you should work before you stop to take a break.

7. Are you going to the bathroom? I'm serious. If you have to go, get up and go. The worst thing is to sit there holding it in.

There's more, but those are the big ones. I think many programmers feel if they get up from their computer it will explode while they're gone. The computer will wait patiently for you to return, and taking breaks gives your brain a chance to work on the problem in a different way.

You should also consider turning on your computer's web camera and record yourself working. You may think you don't slouch, but then in the heat of battle you do some strange things to your body without knowing it. Record yourself this session, and then look for anything causing you tension, problems, or back ache, or that is just weird.

Exercise Challenge

In this exercise you are implementing the `cut` tool. I really like `cut` because it makes me look like a Unix wizard when all it really does is carve streams of text. It is the simplest little text processing tool you could possibly make and still be useful. To work with it you need another tool to feed it some lines of text to carve, so we can do this:

```
ls -l | cut -d ' ' -f 5-7
```

That might give you gibberish, but on most systems it should list the username and group of every file. The `cut` command takes options that set a type of delimiter (`-d ' '` for a space character), and then a list of fields to extract (5–7 in this case). We use the `ls -l` command to give it something to carve up.

That's all there is to it, so read the `man cut` page and see how much of it you can implement while checking out how you keep your body while you work.

Study Drill

What's the impact of unicode on your implementation?

Further Study

Remember, your body is a part of you, and the idea that your mind is all that matters is completely false. Treating your body like it's just useless junk will make your brain work less efficiently and keep you from doing this work comfortably for a long period of time. I recommend you take time to do some kind of physical health–related activity as often as you can. That can be yoga, dance, walking, hiking, or going to the gym. Anything to keep your body healthy so your mind can work without interference.

Think about it this way: If your body is hurt and constantly in discomfort, or weak from abuse, then your brain has to waste cycles on keeping track of it and telling you. If you can keep your body a well-oiled, maintained machine, then your brain doesn't have to worry about it.

Finally, if you are someone whose body doesn't work like other people's, then do the best you can. Nobody is telling you that you have to have my body to be a programmer. One of the great things about coding is anyone can do it even if their physical manifestation can't do many other things. The point is don't let programming make your situation worse. Stay healthy.

sed

U sing these tiny projects to study yourself is useful, but let's pan out and look at the main topics you've focused on:

1. Startup process for beginning work, such as your text editor, how well you can type, and other things that happen inside the computer

2. Mental attitude when you begin and while you work, with a suggestion for journaling as a way to get control over it

3. Work environment including your desk, lighting, chair, and the kind of computer you use

4. Physical posture and health to avoid injuries while you work

In this exercise we'll take this improvement plan and go one step further by tracking some metrics. You have been taking a small command line tool, reading about it and determining its features, and then spending only 45 minutes doing a quick hack. You can now enumerate your features, prioritize them, and then figure out how many you can complete in 45 minutes. In fact, you can go back through all the projects you've done so far and your notes on changes you've made and calculate this metric to see if you've been improving.

Take the time now to go back through your notes and get a rough estimate of the percentage of features you completed for each 45-minute hack. Graph them on some paper, and then look at your notes to see if there were significant changes, *good* or *bad*, when you altered how you work. Then in this exercise try to make a prediction about how much you'll get done based on a change you'll make. You could even try adding some friction *back* to your process and see how that impacts your productivity.

WARNING! Keep in mind that this is a personal metric and not something you should share with anyone else. These are barely even scientific and meant for you to simply gain some objectivity in analyzing how you work. They aren't meant to be grand metrics that can describe all programmers, but you better believe that if a manager finds out you have these they will demand to see them. They will then demand everyone on your team start doing them, and then management will use these to cause you a great deal of trouble. Consider your lab notes a very private journal, and never let anyone see it.

Exercise Challenge

This exercise will get more complicated than the others because we're going to be doing more regular expressions and implementing a tool called sed. The sed utility enables you to alter text by taking a regular expression replacement pattern and then determining what to replace it with in each line it receives. The difficulty may be in implementing sed's expression format, so I recommend you approach this in three ways:

1. Level 1 is having command line options for the most basic sed usage of replacing one string with another.

2. Level 2 is enabling regular expressions in those command line options.

3. Level 3 is implementing the sed expression format.

An example of using sed is to change one word to another in a stream of text. If I wanted to change the output of ls so that my name is replaced by "author" I can do this:

```
ls -l | sed -e "s/zedshaw/author/g"
```

However, the strength of sed lies in doing regular expressions to match patterns and replace them. If you use the vim editor, then you are already familiar with this syntax:

```
ls -l | sed -e "s/Jul [0-9][0-9]/DATE/g"
```

You should read the man sed page, but you may have to do even more research on this to implement it. I suggest you do your research the night before, and then do a 45 minute hack the next day based on that research. This will help you keep your metrics fair and focused on just your work.

Study Drills

1. Did you find out anything unusual or surprising when you compiled your metrics?

2. What was your prediction about your work before you started this session?

3. How did it match what you really did?

Further Study

In the video for this exercise I will show you something called a "run chart." A run chart is a simple graph of some activity you wish to monitor that shows you how it is changing over time. People use run charts to spot big changes in behavior because they are both simple and effective visualization tools. You'll be using run charts more in the book as they are very simple but very powerful.

sort

You are slowly building up what I call a Personal Process Practice (3P), which isn't a new idea at all. The purpose of your 3P is to gain objective insight into how you do things without killing your creativity and productivity. By simply tracking little metrics and making run charts to guide improvements you can drastically change how well you work. The risk though is that this will prevent you from hacking quickly or getting things done or that your 3P will become more work than your real work.

I did this for about four years of my programming career and it worked great to teach me about myself and how I work. It also cut through many of the lies that process advocates push. I had a simple way to actually test if some pundit's views on programming improved my personal productivity. I would say the only mistake I made was taking it much too seriously and killing my creativity for those four years.

This is why you're building an idea of your starting process and work environment in small quick hacks. You don't have time to collect complicated metrics and worry about exactly how you do things when there's only 45 minutes to get something done. Later we'll focus on practices that require concentration, and you'll spend more time and gather slightly better metrics. As you work try not to let the metrics kill your creativity, flow, or well-being. If you hate collecting something, then don't do it. Find a way to automate it, or come up with another metric.

For this exercise you are making a run chart of your percentage of features completed. This means before you work you'll have to enumerate all the features you can find in the standard man pages for the sort command, then mark how many you completed. Remember to sort them so that you can get enough done such that the tool actually works in some way. Getting a 90% score on a tool that doesn't actually sort text means you actually completed 0%.

When you are done you should make the run chart of your feature percentage completed for each project so we can analyze it in the next exercise.

Exercise Challenge

In this exercise you are implementing the sort command, which is a very simple command. It takes lines of text and simply sorts them in order. It does have quite a few options that are interesting, so you should read the man sort page to find out what it can do. Most of the time people just use sort to sort lists of names in order:

```
ls | sort
```

You can also reverse the sort:

```
ls | sort −r
```

And you can control how it sorts, such as ignoring case:

```
ls | sort -f
```

Or, you can even do sorting numerically instead:

```
ls | sort -g
```

This might not really do much to the `ls` output unless it's all numbers.

Your job is to implement as many of these features as you can and keep track of each feature you complete. This should all be in your lab notes so you can analyze it later.

Study Drills

1. Are you at a point now where you've run out of things to improve? Try searching around and looking for other people's process suggestions.

2. We are programmers, people of code. Have you tried to find code that makes you more efficient? My friends Audrey and Danny have a project called cookie-cutter you should check out: https://cookiecutter.readthedocs.io/en/latest/.

3. You should now research how to calculate the mean of a set of numbers. You'll be using this to calculate your run chart middle line using Python.

Further Study

If you really want a correct run chart you'll also need to calculate the `standard deviation` of your numbers. It's not necessary right now but if you want to be technically accurate then this is helpful.

uniq

There isn't much more to say in the beginning of these last two exercises. You should know how to think about your work environment, how you start, how you sit, everything that impacts your ability to get started. You should also have been busting through that initial starting phase using these tiny little 45-minute projects. If you haven't figured it out yet, setting a 45-minute timer and yelling "GO GO GO!" is a solid technique for making yourself get started. The goal hasn't been to craft stellar work but to just get going.

You should also have a decent lab notebook with run charts plotting how well your improvements are working. There's nothing very scientific about your charts, but they should be helping you understand what might be working and what isn't working. When you use a run chart you'll want to simply look for spikes in either direction and then try to find an "assignable cause" for the spike. If the spike was a positive one, then try to find out why and do it again. If the spike was in the negative direction, then try to find out why and prevent it in the future.

When I say "spike" I mean significant changes. One thing about a run chart is it's *supposed* to fluctuate. In fact, if it stays stagnant for a few 45-minute hacks, then that's also bad and you should find out why. Normal processes fluctuate and bounce around the mean, and you should only try to find causes for large spikes in any one direction. If you did the *Further Study* from the previous exercise then you can use $2 * std.dev$ (two times standard deviation) as a line above and below the mean to spot problems.

WARNING! See the video for this exercise for more demonstrations of a run chart. They are much easier to explain visually in a video.

Exercise Challenge

The uniq command simply takes a list of sorted lines from sort and removes any duplicates. It's very handy when you want to get just the unique lines of a list. If you've been implementing these commands then you should be able to do this:

```
history | sed -e "s/^[ 0-9]*//g" | cut -d ' ' -f 1 | sort | uniq
```

The history command prints out a list of every command you've run. Your sed command needs regular expressions and this will strip the beginning off of the history command. Next I use cut to grab just the command name as the first word. After that I sort and run it through uniq, and you have all the commands you run.

Implement enough of uniq and any other commands necessary to make the preceding command work. You can change up the format if your sed can't handle expressions yet, but you should get a list of commands when you're done with this exercise.

Study Drills

1. You now have a list of commands you can start to implement if you want to do further study.

2. This is the first multi-project exercise, where you are combining the exercises from previous steps into one. Did you find anything new about your process?

3. How are your run charts looking? Are they helping?

Further Study

Research charting libraries for Python and see if you can generate these run charts with Python. You should also start tracking how long it takes you to get started and see if the run chart helps you decrease the time it takes.

Review

The first stage of my methodic madness is complete for me but not for you. We are now going to review the strategy of this part of the book so you can continue to use it yourself in the future. The strategy is this:

1. You need to work on that initial start to every project.

2. To isolate this issue you sit down with a set of little projects you can do in 45 minutes. This focuses on the problem area of starting a project and lets you repeat that part of your process.

3. As you work on these projects you identify possible causes of your problem starting a project. This can take the form of your computer setup, work environment, mental thought processes, or physical health. There are more, but those are the big possible causes.

4. Once you've identified possible causes you work on eliminating or changing them within the small confines of your 45 minute hacks.

5. Finally, you record and graph metrics to see if these possible changes are helping but also to make sure they aren't hurting your performance.

This doesn't need to be a formal scientific process to be useful. All you need is to treat this as a journal that helps you objectively view how *you* work. If you're doing it right you'll run into surprising things that you hadn't thought of before. The collection of data forces you to explore new possibilities and expand what you think might be the cause of something.

Please remember that this personal metrics journal should not be shared with others, especially anyone in management. It is innevitable that managers will attempt to impose these metrics on you, and if they do, then you should flat out refuse. These are your personal private notes, and nobody has a right to read them—much like a diary or your private email.

Exercise Challenge

The final exercise is for you to pick your favorite tool and to spend a series of 45-minute sessions refining it over the course of a week or more. Using everything that you've learned about yourself, take this project and start over from scratch to create something more solid. Still limit yourself to 45 minutes at a time, but don't treat this final project as a hack. Instead, it is the next step after a hack that you are working on.

After I'm done hacking on something real quick to test an idea, I will either delete it or clean it. If the hack is so completely disgusting that it should never see the light of day, then I delete it and redo it from a clean beginning. You won't forget the things you did and having to resolve them, but a focus on quality will help you do it cleaner. If the hack isn't so bad, then I'll clean it up before expanding it.

One effective technique for turning a hack into something solid is to extract the key elements of the hack into a library with an automated test suite. This forces you to think about the code as something that will be used in other code. I'll do this:

1. Go through the file and convert my "stream of consciousness hacking" into a set of functions.

2. DRY (Don't Repeat Yourself) up the code a bit, making sure to remove repetition but not too much. Code with zero repetition is basically encrypted randomness.

3. Once it's cleaned up and running the same as before but with functions, I pull those functions out into a module and make sure the original code keeps working. Remember, don't change things while you're cleaning up, just reorganize and fix it.

4. After the code is moved and working again I sit down to write test cases that make sure they keep working for the future when I *do* start changing things.

For this exercise you'll take your favorite of the projects and do this "officializing" process to it. Keep your time to 45 minutes at a time, and go through the above process to clean it up. It's fine to work more than 45 minutes that day, just be sure to take 15-30 minute breaks between each session. It's the same time frame except you're not hacking, you're getting serious.

Study Drills

1. Compare your hack code to your official code. Did you find bugs by cleaning it up? Were there other improvements?

2. If the hack and the cleaned code are nearly the same in behavior, then do you *really* need to clean up the hack? Why would you need to clean up a hack even if it is working just fine and is possibly simpler?

3. Try a new command from your list of commands you run frequently (see Exercise 11), and try this entire process on it. Do a quick hack, then clean it up and make it official.

Further Study

Here is a list of other commands you should attempt doing replicas of in 45 minutes:

- ls
- rm
- rmdir
- mkdir

- `cal`
- `tail`
- `yes`
- `false`

Try implementing some of those.

PART III
Data Structures

You're well on your way to building a personal process that gets you started quickly and with limited friction. Having a good starting process and developing an ability to simply let go and hack is the foundation of creativity. The creative mindset is one of fluidity and relaxation. If you have friction and frustration getting started, then it's difficult to get into the flow. Learning to "click" your brain into creative loose hacking mode helps you solve problems creatively and be more productive.

There is no point being creative if what you make is junk. At first, yes, obviously, the vast majority of what you make will be junk, but you don't want to make terrible software for the rest of your life. You need to balance the creative hacking mentality with a rigorous quality mentality. I advocate that people switch between modes of creative expression and critical thinking. You get your ideas out and realized by being loose and creative, but then you make them tight and high quality by being critical of your own work.

In Part II you actually did this when you tracked the number of features you could complete in 45 minutes and then tried to find places you could improve your starting process. However, you couldn't hack and analyze your process at the same time because the critical thinking mode is a killer to creativity. This advice spans nearly every creative discipline I know and helps you not get in your own way while you work.

> **WARNING!** Criticism during creation kills your imagination. Creativity without criticism produces nothing but garbage. You need both but not at the same time.

In Part III you'll switch gears to focusing on quality and developing personal processes that increase your quality. To keep things simple I am only going to define quality as this:

A low defect rate and understandable code.

Most programmers are absolutely terrible at both of these. The vast majority of developers consider their work completed when the compiler finishes and that's it. They ran the test suite so it's done! I call this "programmer done," where there is no self-critical evaluation of their own work because they totally trust in their computer to find all the defects. They also seem to never care if anyone else can understand their code, focusing only on whether it worked well enough to satisfy the bare minimum. If you were ever to ask them what their daily defect rate is they'd just glare at you and say that's not important. Code coverage? Bah. Their test suite has 100k lines of code! It *must* test everything!

To become a better programmer you must begin the brutal work of looking at your own quality metrics and practices. I say this work is brutal because it demonstrates clearly and obviously exactly how bad you are, and that can be tragic for people who blissfully think they're awesome all the time. Those with impostor syndrome will find this quality analysis refreshing because it will give you a decent idea of how well you're doing and a plan to improve.

Learning Quality through Data Structures

Data structures are a simple enough concept. Your computer has memory and data to put in that memory. You can either stuff it in random places or come up with a structure that makes it easier to process the data. Since the beginning of computer science people have been analyzing exactly how to structure data for different purposes and then how well those structures work. Since data structures are so well defined we can use them to study your quality practices. You will implement each data structure and a test for it and then go through two steps to determine the quality of your implementation.

Your process for doing each of the data structure exercises is as follows:

1. Each exercise will describe the data structure and what you can do with it. This description will be in English, diagrams, and sample code. I'll give a complete description of the structure without code since you are to implement this and get it right.

2. You might have a set of tests that you must pass as well, but these tests might also be written in English, so you'll also be writing an automated test.

3. You'll want to continue your training of doing work in 45-minute bursts with breaks, but you can take more time on each implementation. I recommend you do a few quick hacking sessions, then "get serious" and refine your implementation over more sessions.

4. When you believe you are "done" you'll then switch into critical mode and begin to find out how you *actually* did. You'll follow an auditing process that takes you through your code with a critical eye and looks for bugs, tracking how many you make.

5. Finally, you'll fix your defects found during the audit phase and continue working on the exercise until you're done.

This process is involved, so the first *two* exercises in this part (Exercises 13 and 14) will be done by me, live, with all the defects I make and all the code I have. You'll be able to see how this process works in the videos and read my code in the exercises so you can understand what's expected. I will follow the strict process I outline above as closely as I can, so you'll want to watch the videos carefully.

How to Study Data Structures

There's a formal way to study algorithms and data structures mathematically, but I won't get too far into the theory behind them. If this light introduction interests you then you can read several books on the topic and study this branch of computer science for years and years. In this book I'm going to give you exercises so you can learn how to implement them from memory and understand how they work. You won't need formal proofs for that, just simple Python code and repeated attempts.

With these exercises I want you to follow a specific way to study them so you can implement them from memory. I use this same process when I study music and when I attempt to paint what I see. It works with anything where you need to remember a concept but also apply it creatively to varying situations, so you can't just rote memorize it. Instead you do what I call "memorize, attempt, check":

1.   Set up all the information and material that describes what you have to retain. Do anything you can to memorize it and retain it, even if it's just a small part of the information.

2.   Put *all* of the information away so you can't see it. I like to put it in a different room so I have to get up from my work if I need to look it up again.

3.   Attempt to create, from memory, what you need. Try to put anything down, right or wrong.

4.   When you've exhausted what you could retain, take what you've done and walk back to your information and compare it. Mark off all the things you got wrong and then put your attempt back.

5.   Using your list of errors, focus on memorizing so that you correct the errors on the next attempt and do it all again.

I like to do 2–15 minutes of memorization, then 10–45 minutes of attempts, but you'll know when you've run out of knowledge and need to go get more. I'll give a concrete example by explaining how I paint or draw from memory:

1.   I'm going to paint a flower, so I put the flower in one room of my house and my painting set in another room.

2.   I sit in the flower room and stare at the flower. I do drawings of the flower. I trace it with my finger and try to imagine it in my mind's eye. I visualize myself painting each petal, stem, everything. I remember proportions. I may even write down notes on color and try to mix the colors in the flower room.

3.   *I leave everything in the flower room.* I quickly walk back to the painting room and try to conjure up the memory of the flower to find out what to paint next. Maybe a leaf is finally clear. I paint that. Maybe the pot is clear now, I do some of that. I keep closing my eyes, attempting to remember the image, then try to paint it.

4.   When I'm stuck or I run out of time, I get up and take my little canvas into the flower room and compare it to what I see. I'll then make notes on what I got wrong. Is one petal too long? Is the pot the wrong angle? Is the dirt too dark? I sketch notes and figure out what I got wrong.

5.   Then I take the painting back into the painting room, walk back into the flower room, and use this list of mistakes to continue studying from memory for the next round.

The paintings I make from this process are usually fairly strange but close to the original, depending on how many rounds I take and how often I practice this. Eventually this helped me get better and capture what I see quicker since I could retain more visual information in my memory for longer periods of time.

When you're doing these algorithms exercises you can use the same process to work on your ability to regurgitate them on demand in an interview. You should first just sit down and implement them using all the information you can and learn how they work. It's difficult to memorize something you don't understand. After you have an okay implementation, you can then start to train your memory of it.

1.   Put all the books, notes, diagrams, and information about that algorithm in one room and your laptop in another. Print out your code if you need to.

2.   Spend a good 15 minutes studying the information in your algorithm room, taking notes, drawing more diagrams, visualizing how data flows, and doing anything else you can think of to learn it.

3.   Leaving all that information in the algorithm room, walk into the laptop room and sit down to attempt your implementation from memory. Don't spend more than 45 minutes on this before checking your work.

4.   Walk into the algorithm room with your laptop and take notes (that stay in the algorithm room) on what you got wrong.

5.   Put your laptop back, and then go back into the algorithm room and do another round of memorizing and studying before doing it all again. Focus on all the things you got wrong, and it will make it easier.

The first few times you do this it will be frustrating, but pretty soon you'll find it becomes easier and, in many cases, meditative to work this way.

Single Linked Lists

The first data structure you will implement is the single linked list. I will describe the data structure, list out all the operations you should implement, and give you a single test for your implementation that needs to pass. You should attempt this data structure on your own at first but then watch the video of *my* implementation and the audit afterward so you can understand the process.

WARNING! These are *not* efficiently implemented data structures at all! They are *purposefully* naïve and slow so that we can cover measuring and optimizing data code in Exercises 18 and 19. If you are attempting to use these data structures in professional work, then you will have performance problems.

Description

When dealing with many data structures in an object-oriented language such as Python, you have three common concepts to understand:

1. A "node," which is usually a container or memory location for the data structure. Your values go in here.
2. An "edge," but we'll say "pointer" or "link," that points at other nodes. These are placed inside each node, usually as instance variables.
3. A "controller," which is some class that knows how to use the pointers in a node to structure the data correctly.

In Python we will map these concepts like this:

1. Nodes are just objects defined by a class.
2. Pointers (edges) are just instance variables in the node objects.
3. The controller is simply another class that uses the nodes to store everything and structure the data. This is where all of your operations go (push, pop, list, etc.), and usually the user of the controller never really deals with the nodes or pointers.

In some books on algorithms you'll see implementations that combine the node and controller into one single class or structure, but this is very confusing and also violates separation of concerns in your design. It's better to separate the nodes from the controlling class so that one thing does one thing well and you know where the bugs are.

Imagine we want to store a list of cars in order. We have a first car, which leads to a second, and so on until the end. Imagining this list we can begin to conceive of a node/pointers/controller design for it:

1. Nodes contain each car's description. Maybe it's just a `node.value` variable to a `Car` class. We can call this `SingleLinkedListNode` or `SLLNode` if you're lazy.

2. Each `SLLNode` then has a `next` link to the next node in the chain. Doing `node.next` gets you the next car in the line.

3. A controller simply called `SingleLinkedList` then has operations like `push`, `pop`, `first`, or `count`, which take a `Car` and use nodes to store them internally. When you `push` a `Car` onto the `SingleLinkedList` controller, it works an internal list of linked nodes to store it at the end.

WARNING! Why would we do this when Python has a perfectly good and very fast `list` type? Mostly to learn about data structures is all. In the real world you would just use Python's `list` and move on.

To implement this `SingleLinkedListNode` we'd need a simple class like this:

sllist.py

```
1    class SingleLinkedListNode(object):
2
3        def __init__(self, value, nxt):
4            self.value = value
5            self.next = nxt
6
7        def __repr__(self):
8            nval = self.next and self.next.value or None
9            return f"[{self.value}:{repr(nval)}]"
```

We have to use the word `nxt` since `next` is a reserved word in Python. Other than that, this is a very simple class. The most complicated thing is the `__repr__` function. That just prints debugging output when you use the `''%r''` format, or when you call `repr()` on the node. It should return a string.

WARNING! Take the time now to figure out how to *manually* build a list using just the `SingleLinkedListNode` class and then manually walk through it. This is a good 45-minute hack spike to try at this point in the exercise.

Controller

Once we have our nodes defined in the `SingleLinkedListNode` class we can figure out exactly what the controller should do. Every data structure has a list of common operations you'd need for them to be useful. Different operations take different amounts of memory (space) and time, with some being expensive and others being fast. The structure of the `SingleLinkedListNode` makes some operations very quick but many others very slow. You'll be figuring this out as you work on the implementation.

The easiest way to see the operations is to look at a skeleton version of the `SingleLinkedList` class:

sllist.py

```
1    class SingleLinkedList(object):
2
3        def __init__(self):
4            self.begin = None
5            self.end = None
6
7        def push(self, obj):
8            """Appends a new value on the end of the list."""
9
10       def pop(self):
11           """Removes the last item and returns it."""
12
13       def shift(self, obj):
14           """Another name for push."""
15
16       def unshift(self):
17           """Removes the first item and returns it."""
18
19       def remove(self, obj):
20           """Finds a matching item and removes it from the list."""
21
22       def first(self):
23           """Returns a *reference* to the first item, does not remove."""
24
25       def last(self):
26           """Returns a reference to the last item, does not remove."""
27
28       def count(self):
29           """Counts the number of elements in the list."""
30
31       def get(self, index):
32           """Get the value at index."""
33
34       def dump(self, mark):
35           """Debugging function that dumps the contents of the list."""
```

In other exercises I'll only tell you the operations and leave it for you to figure out, but for this one I'm giving you guidance on implementation. Look through the list of functions in `SingleLinkedList` to see each operation and the comment for how it should work.

Test

I am now going to give you the test that you have to make work when implementing this class. You'll see that I've gone through every operation and tried to cover most of the edge cases, but when I do the audit you'll find out that actually I may have missed a few. It's common that people don't test for cases such as "zero elements" and "one element."

test_sllist.py

```
1    from sllist import *
2
3    def test_push():
4        colors = SingleLinkedList()
5        colors.push("Pthalo Blue")
6        assert colors.count() == 1
7        colors.push("Ultramarine Blue")
8        assert colors.count() == 2
9
10   def test_pop():
11       colors = SingleLinkedList()
12       colors.push("Magenta")
13       colors.push("Alizarin")
14       assert colors.pop() == "Alizarin"
15       assert colors.pop() == "Magenta"
16       assert colors.pop() == None
17
18   def test_unshift():
19       colors = SingleLinkedList()
20       colors.push("Viridian")
21       colors.push("Sap Green")
22       colors.push("Van Dyke")
23       assert colors.unshift() == "Viridian"
24       assert colors.unshift() == "Sap Green"
25       assert colors.unshift() == "Van Dyke"
26       assert colors.unshift() == None
27
28   def test_shift():
29       colors = SingleLinkedList()
30       colors.shift("Cadmium Orange")
31       assert colors.count() == 1
32
33       colors.shift("Carbazole Violet")
34       assert colors.count() == 2
35
36       assert colors.pop() == "Cadmium Orange"
37       assert colors.count() == 1
38       assert colors.pop() == "Carbazole Violet"
39       assert colors.count() == 0
40
41   def test_remove():
42       colors = SingleLinkedList()
43       colors.push("Cobalt")
```

```
44          colors.push("Zinc White")
45          colors.push("Nickle Yellow")
46          colors.push("Perinone")
47          assert colors.remove("Cobalt") == 0
48          colors.dump("before perinone")
49          assert colors.remove("Perinone") == 2
50          colors.dump("after perinone")
51          assert colors.remove("Nickle Yellow") == 1
52          assert colors.remove("Zinc White") == 0
53
54      def test_first():
55          colors = SingleLinkedList()
56          colors.push("Cadmium Red Light")
57          assert colors.first() == "Cadmium Red Light"
58          colors.push("Hansa Yellow")
59          assert colors.first() == "Cadmium Red Light"
60          colors.shift("Pthalo Green")
61          assert colors.first() == "Pthalo Green"
62
63      def test_last():
64          colors = SingleLinkedList()
65          colors.push("Cadmium Red Light")
66          assert colors.last() == "Cadmium Red Light"
67          colors.push("Hansa Yellow")
68          assert colors.last() == "Hansa Yellow"
69          colors.shift("Pthalo Green")
70          assert colors.last() == "Hansa Yellow"
71
72      def test_get():
73          colors = SingleLinkedList()
74          colors.push("Vermillion")
75          assert colors.get(0) == "Vermillion"
76          colors.push("Sap Green")
77          assert colors.get(0) == "Vermillion"
78          assert colors.get(1) == "Sap Green"
79          colors.push("Cadmium Yellow Light")
80          assert colors.get(0) == "Vermillion"
81          assert colors.get(1) == "Sap Green"
82          assert colors.get(2) == "Cadmium Yellow Light"
83          assert colors.pop() == "Cadmium Yellow Light"
84          assert colors.get(0) == "Vermillion"
85          assert colors.get(1) == "Sap Green"
86          assert colors.get(2) == None
87          colors.pop()
88          assert colors.get(0) == "Vermillion"
89          colors.pop()
90          assert colors.get(0) == None
```

Study this test carefully so that you have a good idea of how each operation *should* work before trying
to implement it. I wouldn't write all of this code into a file at once. Instead it's better to do just one test at
a time and make it work in small chunks.

WARNING! At this point if you are unfamiliar with automated testing then you will want to watch the video to watch me do it.

Introductory Auditing

As you make each test run you will conduct an audit of your code to find defects. Eventually you will track the number of defects you find with your audits, but for now you're going to just practice auditing code after you write it. An "audit" is similar to what a tax agent does when the government thinks you are cheating on your taxes. They go through each transaction, each amount of money coming in, all money going out, and why you spent it the way you did. A code audit is similar as you go through each function, and analyze all parameters coming in, and all values going out.

To conduct a basic audit you will do this:

1.   Start at the top of your test case. Let's do `test_push` in this example.

2.   Look at the first code line and determine what is being called and what is being created. In this case it's `colors = SingleLinkedList()`. That means we are creating a `colors` variable, and calling the `SingleLinkedList.__init__` function.

3.   Jump to the top of this `__init__` function, keeping your test case and the target function (`__init__`) side by side. Confirm that you have done so. You then confirm that you called it with the *correct number and type of function arguments*. In this case `__init__` only takes `self`, and it should be the right type.

4.   You then go into `__init__` and go line by line, confirming each function call and variable in the same way. Does it have the right number of arguments? The right types?

5.   At each branch (`if-statement`, `for-loop`, `while-loop`) you confirm that the logic is correct and that it handles any possible conditions in the logic. Do `if-statements` have `else` clauses with errors? Do `while-loops` end? Then dive into each branch and track the functions the same way, diving in, checking variables, and coming back, checking returns.

6.   When you get to the end of a function or any `return`, you jump back to the `test_push` caller to check that what *is* returned matches what you expect when you called it. Remember, though, that you do this for each call in `__ini__` as well.

7.   You are done when you reach the end of the `test_push` function and you've done this recursive checking into and out of each function it calls.

This process seems tedious at first, and yes it is, but you'll get quicker at it the more often you do it. In the video you'll see me do this *before* I run each test (or at least I try really hard to do it). I follow the following process:

1.   Write some test code.

2.   Write the code to make the test work.

3.   Audit both.

4.   Run the test to see if I was right.

Exercise Challenge

We now reach the part where you're ready to try this. First, read through the test and study what it does, and study the code in `sllist.py` to figure out what you need to do. I suggest that when you attempt to implement a function in `SingleLinkedList` you first write the comments describing what it does, then fill in the Python code to make those comments work. You'll see me do this in the video.

When you have spent one or two 45-minute sessions hacking on this and trying to make it work, it's time to watch the video. You'll want to attempt it first so that you have a better idea of what I'm trying to do, which makes the video easier to understand. The video will be me just coding and not talking, but I'll do a voice-over to discuss what's going on. The video will also be faster to save time, and I'll edit out any boring mistakes or wasted time.

Once you see how I do it, and you've taken notes (right?), then go and attempt your more serious tries and perform the code auditing process as carefully as you can.

Auditing

Once you have written your code, make sure you do the auditing process I describe in the introduction to Part III. I will also be doing it in the video for this exercise if you aren't quite sure how it's done.

Study Drill

Your study drill for this exercise is to try to implement this algorithm *again*, completely from memory the way I describe in the introduction to Part III. You should also try to think through what operations in this data structure are most likely painfully slow. When you are done, perform your auditing process on what you created.

Double Linked Lists

The previous exercise may have taken you quite a while to complete since you have to figure out how to make a single linked list work. Hopefully, the video gave you enough information to complete the exercise and also showed you exactly how to do an audit of your code. In this exercise you're going to implement the better version of linked lists called DoubleLinkedList.

In the SingleLinkedList you should have realized that any operation involving the end of the list has to travel through each node until it gets to the end. A SingleLinkedList is only efficient from the front of the list where you can easily change the next pointer. The shift and unshift operations are fast, but pop and push cost you as the list gets bigger. You *might* be able to speed this up by keeping a reference to the next-to-last element, but then what if you want to replace that element? Again, you'll have to go through all of the elements to find this one. You can get some speed improvements with a few minor changes like this, but a better solution is to simply change the structure to make it easier to work from any position.

The DoubleLinkedList is nearly the same as the SingleLinkedList except it also has a prev (for previous) link to the DoubleLinkedListNode that comes before it. One extra pointer per node and suddenly many of the operations become much easier. You can also easily add a pointer to the end in the DoubleLinkedList so you have direct access to both the beginning and the end. This makes push and pop efficient again since you can access the end directly and use the node.prev pointer to get the previous node.

With these changes in mind our node class looks like this:

dllist.py

```
1    class DoubleLinkedListNode(object):
2
3        def __init__(self, value, nxt, prev):
4            self.value = value
5            self.next = nxt
6            self.prev = prev
7
8        def __repr__(self):
9            nval = self.next and self.next.value or None
10           pval = self.prev and self.prev.value or None
11           return f"[{self.value}, {repr(nval)}, {repr(pval)}]"
```

All that's added is the self.prev = prev line and then handling that in the __repr__ function. Implementing the DoubleLinkedList class uses the same operations as the SingleLinkedList class, except you add one more variable for the end of the list:

dllist.py

```
1   class DoubleLinkedList(object):
2
3       def __init__(self):
4           self.begin = None
5           self.end = None
```

Introducing Invariant Conditions

All of the operations to implement are the same, but *now* we have some additional considerations:

dllist.py

```
1        def push(self, obj):
2            """Appends a new value on the end of the list."""
3
4        def pop(self):
5            """Removes the last item and returns it."""
6
7        def shift(self, obj):
8            """Actually just another name for push."""
9
10       def unshift(self):
11           """Removes the first item (from begin) and returns it."""
12
13       def detach_node(self, node):
14           """You'll need to use this operation sometimes, but mostly
15           inside remove().  It should take a node, and detach it from the
16           list, whether the node is at the front, end, or in the middle."""
17
18       def remove(self, obj):
19           """Finds a matching item and removes it from the list."""
20
21       def first(self):
22           """Returns a *reference* to the first item, does not remove."""
23
24       def last(self):
25           """Returns a reference to the last item, does not remove."""
26
27       def count(self):
28           """Counts the number of elements in the list."""
29
30       def get(self, index):
31           """Get the value at index."""
32
33       def dump(self, mark):
34           """Debugging function that dumps the contents of the list."""
```

With a `prev` pointer you now have to handle more conditions in each operation:

1. Are there zero elements? Then `self.begin` and `self.end` need to be None.

2. If there is one element, then `self.begin` and `self.end` have to be equal (point at same node).

3. The first element must always have a `prev` that is None.

4. The last element must always have a `next` that is None.

These truths have to hold during the life of the `DoubleLinkedList`, which makes them "invariant conditions" or just "invariants." The idea of an invariant is that, no matter what, these are base checks that show the structure is working correctly. A way to look at invariants is any tests or `assert` calls you seem to do repeatedly can be moved into a special function called `_invariant` which does these checks. You can then call this function in your tests or at the beginning and end of each function. Doing that will cut down on your defect rates since you are saying, "No matter what I do, these have to be true."

The only problem with invariant checks is they can cost time to run. If every function call also calls another function twice then you are adding a potentially significant burden to every function. If your invariant function also does something costly it gets worse. Imagine if you added the invariant: "All nodes have a `next` and `prev` except the first and last ones." That would mean every function call does a complete traversal through the list *twice*. When you have to make sure the class works all the time, this is worth it. If you don't, then it becomes a problem.

In this book you'll use invariant functions when you can, but keep in mind that they aren't something you *always* need to use. Finding ways to only activate them in test suites or debugging or using them during initial development is the key to using them effectively. I recommend that you only call invariants at the tops of functions or only call them inside the test suite. This is a good compromise.

Exercise Challenge

In this exercise you'll implement the operations for the `DoubleLinkedList`, but this time you'll also use an `_invariant` function to check that it is working correctly before and after each operation. The best way to do this is to call the invariant at the top of each function and then in the test suite at key spots. Your test suite for the `DoubleLinkedList` is almost a copy-paste replica of the `SingleLinkedList` test, except you are adding `_invariant` calls at key points.

As with the `SingleLinkedList` you'll want to manually study this data structure on your own. You should draw out the node structures on paper and do some of the operations manually. Next, work the `DoubleLinkedListNode` manually in your `dllist.py` file. After that spend one or two 45-minute sessions trying to hack up a few operations to figure it out. I recommend `push` and `pop`. After that you can watch the video to see me work on it and how I use a combination of auditing my code and the `_invariant` function to check what I'm doing.

Study Drill

As with the previous exercise you'll want to implement this data structure *again* from memory. Put what you know about it in one room and your laptop in another room. You'll want to do this until you can implement the `DoubleLinkedList` from memory without reference.

Stacks and Queues

When working with data structures you'll oftentimes encounter a structure that is similar to another. A Stack is similar to a SingleLinkedList from Exercise 13, and a Queue is similar to a DoubleLinkedList from Exercise 14. The only difference is a Stack and a Queue restrict the possible operations to simplify how they are used. This helps reduce defects since you can't accidentally use the Stack like a Queue and cause problems. In a Stack, the nodes are "pushed" onto the "top" and then "popped" from the top as well. With a Queue, the nodes are shifted to the "tail" and then unshifted off the "head" of the structure. Both of these operations are simply simplifications of the SingleLinkedList and DoubleLinkedList where a Stack only allows push and pop while a Queue only allows shift and unshift.

When visualizing the Stack you should think of a stack of books on your floor. Think really heavy art books like the kind I have on my bookshelf that, if I stacked 20 of them, would probably weigh about 100 pounds. When you build this stack of books, you don't lift up the whole stack and put the books on the bottom, right? No, you put the books on the *top* of the stack. You drop them, but we can use the word "push" for this action too. If you wanted to get a book from the stack, you could probably lift some of them and grab one, but ultimately you'd probably have to take some from the top to get to the ones at the bottom. You would lift up each book from the *top*, or in our case we'd say "pop one off the top." This is how a Stack works, and if you think about it, that's just a linked list of books forced into a line by gravity.

Visualizing a Queue is easiest if you think of waiting in line at the bank with a "head" and "tail" on the line. Usually there's a rope maze that has an entrance at the end and an exit where the tellers are located. You enter the queue by entering the "tail" of this rope maze line, and we'll call that shift because that's a common programming word in the Queue data structure. Once you enter the bank line (queue), you can't just jump the line and leave or else people will get mad. So you wait, and as each person in front of you exits the line you get closer to exiting from the "head." Once you reach the end then you can exit, and we'll call that unshift. A Queue is therefore similar to a DoubleLinkedList because you are working from *both* ends of the data structure.

Many times you can find real-world examples of a data structure to help you visualize how it works. You should take the time now to draw these scenarios or actually get a stack of books and test out the operations. How many other real situations can you find that are similar to a Stack and a Queue?

Exercise Challenge

I am now going to ween you off of code-based exercise challenges and have you implement data structures from descriptions of them. In this challenge you are first expected to implement a Stack data structure using the starter code here and what you know about the SingleLinkedList from Exercise 13. Once you've done that, you're going to attempt to make the Queue data structure from nothing.

The StackNode node class is nearly identical to the SingleLinkedListNode, and in fact I just copied it over and changed the name:

stack.py

```
1    class StackNode(object):
2
3        def __init__(self, value, nxt):
4            self.value = value
5            self.next = nxt
6
7        def __repr__(self):
8            nval = self.next and self.next.value or None
9            return f"[{self.value}:{repr(nval)}]"
```

The Stack control class is also very similar to the SingleLinkedList except I use top instead of first. That matches with the concept of a Stack.

stack.py

```
1    class Stack(object):
2
3        def __init__(self):
4            self.top = None
5
6        def push(self, obj):
7            """Pushes a new value to the top of the stack."""
8
9        def pop(self):
10           """Pops the value that is currently on the top of the stack."""
11
12       def top(self):
13           """Returns a *reference* to the first item, does not remove."""
14
15       def count(self):
16           """Counts the number of elements in the stack."""
17
18       def dump(self, mark="----"):
19           """Debugging function that dumps the contents of the stack."""
```

Your challenge is to now implement the Stack and also write a test for it similar to the tests you did in Exercise 13. Make sure your test covers every operation in every way that you can. Remember, though, that push on the stack has to go on the top, so have a link to the top.

Once you have a working Stack you should implement the Queue but base it on the DoubleLinkedList. What you learned from the Stack should be that you can keep the same basic internal structure as a SingleLinkedList but just change the allowed functions. With a Queue it's the same thing. Take the time to diagram and visualize how a Queue works, then figure out how it restricts the DoubleLinkedList. Once you have that, create your Queue.

Breaking It

Breaking these data structures is simply a matter of not maintaining discipline. See what happens if one operation fails to use the correct end.

You may also have noticed that there's a constant risk of an "off by one" error. In my design, I set `self.top` = None for when the structure is empty. This means when you reach 0 elements, you have to do some juggling of `self.top`. An alternative is to make `self.top` always point at a `StackNode` (or any node) and to say the structure is empty when you have this last element. Try this out and see how that changes your implementation. Is that more or less error prone?

Further Study

There are many operations for these data structures that are horribly inefficient. Go back through the code you've written for every data structure and try to guess which of those functions are slowest. Once you have an idea, try to explain why they might be very slow. Research what other people might say about these data structures as well. In Exercises 18 and 19 you'll learn to do some performance analysis of these data structures and tune them.

Finally, did you *really* need to implement a whole new data structure, or could you have simply "wrapped" the `SingleLinkedList` and `DoubleLinkedList` data structures? How does this change your design?

Bubble, Quick, and Merge Sort

You are now going to attempt to implement sorting algorithms for your `DoubleLinkedList` data structure. For these descriptions I'm going to use a "list of numbers" to mean a randomized list of things. This could be a deck of poker cards, sheets of paper with numbers on them, lists of names, or anything else you can sort. There are three usual suspects when you're attempting to sort a list of numbers:

Bubble Sort   This is most likely how you would attempt to sort a list of numbers if you knew nothing about sorting. It involves simply going through the list and swapping any out-of-order pairs you find. You continually loop through the list, swapping pairs, until you've gone through without swapping anything. It's simple to understand, but *crazy* slow.

Merge Sort   This kind of sorting algorithm divides the list into halves, then quarters, and further partitions until it can't divide it anymore. Then it merges these back, but does it in the right order by checking the ordering of each partition as it merges it. It's a clever algorithm that works really well on linked lists but isn't so great on fixed size arrays as you'll need a `Queue` of some kind to keep track of the partitions.

Quick Sort   This is similar to merge sort since it's a "divide and conquer" algorithm, but it works by swapping elements around the partition point instead of breaking and merging the list together. In the simplest form, you pick a range from low to high and a partition point. You then swap the elements that are greater than the partition point above it and those lower below it. Then you pick a new low, high, and partition that's inside this newly shuffled set and do it again. It's dividing the list into smaller chunks, but it doesn't break them apart like a merge sort does.

Exercise Challenge

The purpose of this exercise is to learn how to implement an algorithm based on a "pseudo-code" description or "p-code." You'll be studying the algorithms in references I tell you (primarily Wikipedia) and then using the p-code to implement them. I'll do the first two quickly here and more elaborately in the videos for this exercise. Then your job is to do the quick sort algorithm on your own. First, let's look at the description of the bubble sort from Wikipedia (https://en.wikipedia.org/wiki/Bubble_sort) to get started:

```
procedure bubbleSort( A : list of sortable items )
    n = length(A)
    repeat
        swapped = false
        for i = 1 to n-1 inclusive do
            /* if this pair is out of order */
```

```
            if A[i-1] > A[i] then
                /* swap them and remember something changed */
                swap( A[i-1], A[i] )
                swapped = true
            end if
        end for
    until not swapped
end procedure
```

You'll find that because p-code is just a loose description of the algorithm, it will end up being wildly different between books, authors, and pages on Wikipedia. It's assumed that you can read this "programming-like language" and translate it to what you want. Sometimes the language will look like an old language called Algol; other times it'll look like poorly formatted JavaScript or Python. You just have to try to guess at what it's saying and then translate it to what you need. Here's my initial implementation of this particular p-code:

sorting.py

```
1    def bubble_sort(numbers):
2        """Sorts a list of numbers using bubble sort."""
3        while True:
4            # start off assuming it's sorted
5            is_sorted = True
6            # comparing 2 at a time, skipping ahead
7            node = numbers.begin.next
8            while node:
9                # loop through comparing node to the next
10               if node.prev.value > node.value:
11                   # if the next is greater, then we need to swap
12                   node.prev.value, node.value = node.value, node.prev.value
13                   # oops, looks like we have to scan again
14                   is_sorted = False
15               node = node.next
16
17           # this is reset at the top but if we never swapped, it's sorted
18           if is_sorted: break
```

I've added additional comments here so you can study this and follow along, comparing what I've done here to the p-code. You should also see that the Wikipedia page is using a completely different data structure from your `DoubleLinkedList`. The Wikipedia code is assuming some sort of functioning array or list structure. You have to translate lines such as

```
    if A[i-1] > A[i] then
```

into Python using your `DoubleLinkedList`:

```
    if node.prev.value > node.value:
```

We can't randomly access a `DoubleLinkedList` easily, so we have to convert these array index operations into `.next` and `.prev`. We also have to watch for the next or prev attributes being None while we loop. This kind of conversion requires a lot of translation, study, and guessing at the semantics of the p-code you're reading.

Study Bubble Sort

You should now take the time to study this `bubble_sort` Python code to see how I translated it. Be sure to watch the video so you can watch me do it in real time and get more insight. You should also draw diagrams of how this works on different kinds of lists (already sorted, random, duplicates, etc). Once you have an understanding of how I did it, study the `pytest` for this and the `merge_sort` algorithm:

test_sorting.py

```python
1    import sorting
2    from dllist import DoubleLinkedList
3    from random import randint
4
5    max_numbers = 30
6
7    def random_list(count):
8        numbers = DoubleLinkedList()
9        for i in range(count, 0, -1):
10           numbers.shift(randint(0, 10000))
11       return numbers
12
13
14   def is_sorted(numbers):
15       node = numbers.begin
16       while node and node.next:
17           if node.value > node.next.value:
18               return False
19           else:
20               node = node.next
21
22       return True
23
24
25   def test_bubble_sort():
26       numbers = random_list(max_numbers)
27
28       sorting.bubble_sort(numbers)
29
30       assert is_sorted(numbers)
31
32
33   def test_merge_sort():
34       numbers = random_list(max_numbers)
35
36       sorting.merge_sort(numbers)
37
38       assert is_sorted(numbers)
```

An important part of this test code is that I'm using the `random.randint` function to generate randomized data for testing. This test doesn't test for many edge cases, but it's a start, and we'll be improving it later. Remember that you don't have `sorting.merge_sort` implemented yet, so you can either not write that test function or comment it out for now.

Once you have the test and this code written up, study the Wikipedia page again and attempt some of the other versions of `bubble_sort` before attempting `merge_sort`.

Merge Sort

I'm not quite ready to leave you on your own yet. I'm going to have you repeat this process again for the `merge_sort` function, but this time I want you to attempt to solve the algorithm from just the p-code on the merge sort Wikipedia page (https://en.wikipedia.org/wiki/Merge_sort) *before* you look at how I did it. There are several proposed implementations, but I used the "top down" version:

```
function merge_sort(list m)
    if length of m ≤ 1 then
        return m

    var left := empty list
    var right := empty list
    for each x with index i in m do
        if i < (length of m)/2 then
            add x to left
        else
            add x to right

    left := merge_sort(left)
    right := merge_sort(right)

    return merge(left, right)

function merge(left, right)
    var result := empty list

    while left is not empty and right is not empty do
        if first(left) ≤ first(right) then
            append first(left) to result
            left := rest(left)
        else
            append first(right) to result
            right := rest(right)

    while left is not empty do
        append first(left) to result
        left := rest(left)
    while right is not empty do
        append first(right) to result
```

```
        right := rest(right)
    return result
```

Write the remaining test case function for `test_merge_sort`, and then make an attempt at this implementation. One clue I will give you is that this algorithm works best when given *only* the first `DoubleLinkedListNode`. You'll also probably need a way to count the number of nodes from just a given node. That's something the `DoubleLinkedList` doesn't do.

Merge Sort Cheat Mode

If you attempted it for a while and need to cheat, here's what I did:

sorting.py

```
 1    def count(node):
 2        count = 0
 3
 4        while node:
 5            node = node.next
 6            count += 1
 7
 8        return count
 9
10
11    def merge_sort(numbers):
12        numbers.begin = merge_node(numbers.begin)
13
14        # horrible way to get the end
15        node = numbers.begin
16        while node.next:
17            node = node.next
18        numbers.end = node
19
20
21    def merge_node(start):
22        """Sorts a list of numbers using merge sort."""
23        if start.next == None:
24            return start
25
26        mid = count(start) // 2
27
28        # scan to the middle
29        scanner = start
30        for i in range(0, mid-1):
31            scanner = scanner.next
32
33        # set mid node right after the scan point
34        mid_node = scanner.next
35        # break at the mid point
```

```
36          scanner.next = None
37          mid_node.prev = None
38
39          merged_left = merge_node(start)
40          merged_right = merge_node(mid_node)
41
42          return merge(merged_left, merged_right)
43
44
45
46     def merge(left, right):
47          """Performs the merge of two lists."""
48          result = None
49
50          if left == None: return right
51          if right == None: return left
52
53          if left.value > right.value:
54              result = right
55              result.next = merge(left, right.next)
56          else:
57              result = left
58              result.next = merge(left.next, right)
59
60          result.next.prev = result
61          return result
```

I would use this code as a "cheat sheet" to get quick clues while attempting your implementation. You'll also see me in the video attempt to re-implement this code from scratch, so you can watch me struggle with the same issues you are probably having.

Quick Sort

Finally, it's your turn to attempt the `quick_sort` implementation and to create a `test_quicksort` test case. I recommend you *first* implement a simple quick sort using just Python's normal `list` types. This will help you understand it better. Then, take your simple Python code and make it use the `DoubleLinkedList`. Remember to take your time working this out and, obviously, do lots of debugging and tests in your `test_quicksort`.

Study Drills

1. These implementations are definitely *not* the best when it comes to performance. Try to write some *heinous* tests that demonstrate this. You may need to throw a large list at the algorithms. Use your research to find out what pathological (absolute worst) cases exist. For example, what happens when you give `quick_sort` an already sorted list?

2.   Don't implement any improvements yet, but research various improvements you can make to these algorithms.

3.   Find other sorting algorithms and try to implement them.

4.   Do these also work on `SingleLinkedList`? What about `Queue` and `Stack`? Is this useful?

5.   Read about the theoretical speed of these algorithms. You'll see references to $O(n^2)$ or $O(n\ log\ n)$, which is a way of saying that in the worst case these algorithms will perform that poorly. Determining the "Big-O" for an algorithm is beyond the scope of this book, but we'll discuss these measurements briefly in Exercise 18.

6.   I implemented these as a separate module, but would it be simpler to add them as functions on `DoubleLinkedList`? If you do, then would you need to copy that code to the other data structures it can work on? We're not at a design decision for how to make these sorting algorithms work with any "linked list–like data structure."

7.   Never use bubble sort again. I've included it here because you'll run into it often in bad code and because we'll be improving the performance in Exercise 19.

Dictionary

You should be familiar with Python's `dict` class already. Any time you write code like

```
cars = {'Toyota': 4, 'BMW': 20, 'Audi': 10}
```

you're using a `dict` to associate the models of cars (`'Toyota'`, `'BMW'`, `'Audi'`) to the total you have (`4`, `20`, `10`). Using this data structure should be second nature to you by now, and you probably don't even think about how it works. In this exercise you will learn how a `dict` works by implementing your very own `Dictionary` from data structures you already created. Your goal in this exercise is to implement your own version of a `Dictionary` based on code I've written here.

Exercise Challenge

In this exercise you are going to fully document and understand a piece of code I've written and then write your own version of it from memory as best you can. The purpose of this exercise is to learn to dissect and understand a complicated piece of code. It is also important to be able to internalize, or memorize, what goes into creating a simple data structure like a `Dictionary`. The best way I've found to learn to dissect and understand a piece of code is to reimplement it based on your own study and memorization.

Think of this as a "master copy" class. A master copy comes from painting, where you take a painting created by someone better than you and attempt to make a copy of it. Doing this teaches you how that person painted and improves your skills. Code and paintings are similar in that all the information is right there ready to copy, so you can easily learn from someone else by just copying their work.

Doing a "Code Master Copy"

To create a "code master copy" you'll follow this procedure, which I'm calling the CASMIR process:

1. *Copy* the code and get it working like you normally do. Your copy should be *exactly* the same. This helps you get an understanding of it and forces you to study it closely.

2. *Annotate* the code with comments and write an analysis for all of the code, making sure you understand every line and what it does. This may involve jumping into other code you've written to tie the whole concept together.

3. *Summarize* the general structure with succinct notes for what makes this code work. That would be a list of functions and what each function does.

4. *Memorize* this succinct description of the algorithm and key pieces of code.

5. *Implement* what you can from memory, and when you run out of details, go back to your notes and original code to memorize more.

6. *Repeat* this process as many times as you need to finally make a copy from memory. Your copy from memory does *not* have to be exactly the same but should be close and pass the same test you create.

Doing this will give you a deeper understanding of how the data structure works but, more importantly, will also help you internalize and recall what this data structure does. You'll be able to understand the concept and also implement the data structure when you need to create one. This will *also* train your brain to memorize other data structures and algorithms in the future.

WARNING! The *only* warning I have is that this is a very naïve, stupid, slow implementation of a Dictionary. You are really copying a simplified stupid Dictionary that has all the basic elements and works but needs vast improvements for production. Those improvements will come when we reach Exercise 19 and study performance tuning. For now, just implement this simple version so you can understand the basics of the data structure.

Copy the Code

First we'll look at the code for Dictionary that you'll have to copy:

dictionary.py

```
1    from dllist import DoubleLinkedList
2
3    class Dictionary(object):
4        def __init__(self, num_buckets=256):
5            """Initializes a Map with the given number of buckets."""
6            self.map = DoubleLinkedList()
7            for i in range(0, num_buckets):
8                self.map.push(DoubleLinkedList())
9
10       def hash_key(self, key):
11           """Given a key this will create a number and then convert it to
12           an index for the aMap's buckets."""
13           return hash(key) % self.map.count()
14
15       def get_bucket(self, key):
16           """Given a key, find the bucket where it would go."""
17           bucket_id = self.hash_key(key)
18           return self.map.get(bucket_id)
19
```

```
20      def get_slot(self, key, default=None):
21          """
22          Returns either the bucket and node for a slot, or None, None
23          """
24          bucket = self.get_bucket(key)
25
26          if bucket:
27              node = bucket.begin
28              i = 0
29
30              while node:
31                  if key == node.value[0]:
32                      return bucket, node
33                  else:
34                      node = node.next
35                      i += 1
36
37          # fall through for both if and while above
38          return bucket, None
39
40      def get(self, key, default=None):
41          """Gets the value in a bucket for a given key, or the default."""
42          bucket, node = self.get_slot(key, default=default)
43          return node and node.value[1] or node
44
45      def set(self, key, value):
46          """Sets the key to the value, replacing any existing value."""
47          bucket, slot = self.get_slot(key)
48
49          if slot:
50              # the key exists, replace it
51              slot.value = (key, value)
52          else:
53              # the key does not, append to create it
54              bucket.push((key, value))
55
56      def delete(self, key):
57          """Deletes the given key from the Map."""
58          bucket = self.get_bucket(key)
59          node = bucket.begin
60
61          while node:
62              k, v = node.value
63              if key == k:
64                  bucket.detach_node(node)
65                  break
66
67      def list(self):
68          """Prints out what's in the Map."""
69          bucket_node = self.map.begin
```

```
70              while bucket_node:
71                  slot_node = bucket_node.value.begin
72                  while slot_node:
73                      print(slot_node.value)
74                      slot_node = slot_node.next
75                  bucket_node = bucket_node.next
```

This code implements a `dict` data structure using your existing `DoubleLinkedList` code. If you don't fully understand the `DoubleLinkedList` then you should attempt the code master copy procedure I give you to understand it better. Once you're sure you understand `DoubleLinkedList` you can type this code in and get it working. Remember that it *must* be a perfect copy before you start to annotate it. The worst thing you could do is annotate a broken or incorrect copy of my code.

To help you get this code right, I've written a quick and dirty little test script:

test_dictionary.py

```
1   from dictionary import Dictionary
2
3   # create a mapping of state to abbreviation
4   states = Dictionary()
5   states.set('Oregon', 'OR')
6   states.set('Florida', 'FL')
7   states.set('California', 'CA')
8   states.set('New York', 'NY')
9   states.set('Michigan', 'MI')
10
11  # create a basic set of states and some cities in them
12  cities = Dictionary()
13  cities.set('CA', 'San Francisco')
14  cities.set('MI', 'Detroit')
15  cities.set('FL', 'Jacksonville')
16
17  # add some more cities
18  cities.set('NY', 'New York')
19  cities.set('OR', 'Portland')
20
21
22  # print(out some cities
23  print('-' * 10)
24  print("NY State has: %s" % cities.get('NY'))
25  print("OR State has: %s" % cities.get('OR'))
26
27  # print(some states
28  print('-' * 10)
29  print("Michigan's abbreviation is: %s" % states.get('Michigan'))
30  print("Florida's abbreviation is: %s" % states.get('Florida'))
31
32  # do it by using the state then cities dict
33  print('-' * 10)
```

```
34    print("Michigan has: %s" % cities.get(states.get('Michigan')))
35    print("Florida has: %s" % cities.get(states.get('Florida')))
36
37    # print(every state abbreviation
38    print('-' * 10)
39    states.list()
40
41    # print(every city in state
42    print('-' * 10)
43    cities.list()
44
45    print('-' * 10)
46    state = states.get('Texas')
47
48    if not state:
49      print("Sorry, no Texas.")
50
51    # default values using ||= with the nil result
52    # can you do this on one line?
53    city = cities.get('TX', 'Does Not Exist')
54    print("The city for the state 'TX' is: %s" % city)
```

I want you to also type this code in *exactly*, but when you move on to the next phase of the master copy you'll turn this into an official automated test you can run with pytest. For now, just get this script working so you can get the Dictionary class working, then you can clean it all up in the next phase.

Annotate the Code

Make sure your copy of my code is exactly the same and that it passes the test script. You can then start annotating the code and studying every line to understand what each line does. A very good way to do this is to write an "official" automated test and annotate the code as you work. Take the dictionary_test.py script and convert each section into a little test function, then annotate the Dictionary class as you go.

For example, the first section of the test in test_dictionary.py creates a dictionary and does a series of Dictionary.set calls. I would convert that to a test_set function and then annotate the Dictionary.set function in the dictionary.py file. As you annotate the Dictionary.set function, you'll have to dive into the Dictionary.get_slot function, then the Dictionary.get_bucket function, and finally Dictionary.hash_key. This forces you to annotate and understand a large chunk of the Dictionary class with just one test and in an organized way.

Summarize the Data Structure

You can now summarize what you've learned from annotating the code in dictionary.py and rewriting the dictionary_test.py file to be a real pytest automated test. Your summary should be a clear and short description of the data structure. If you can fit it on a piece of paper then you're doing well. Not all data structures can be summarized that concisely, but keeping the summary small will help you memorize it. You can use diagrams, drawings, words, or whatever you'll be able to remember.

The purpose of this summary is to give you a set of quick notes that you can "hang" more details on when you memorize in the next step. The summary doesn't have to include everything but should include little bits that trigger your memories of the code from the "annotate" phase, which should in turn trigger your memories of the "copy" phase. This is called "chunking," where you attach more detailed memories and information to small pieces of information. Keep this in mind when you're writing the summary. Less is more, but too little is useless.

Memorize the Summary

You're going to memorize the summary and annotated code any way you can, but I'm going to give a basic process for memorizing you can use at first. Honestly, memorizing complex things is an organic trial and error process for everyone, but some tricks help:

1. Make sure you have a pad of paper and printouts of the summary and code.

2. Spend three minutes simply reading the summary and trying to remember it. Quietly stare at it, read it out loud, read it then close your eyes and repeat what you read, and even try just remembering the "shape" of the words on the paper. It sounds nuts but trust me, it totally works. Your brain is better at remembering shapes than you think.

3. Flip the summary over and try to write it again from what you remember, and when you get stuck, flip the summary over real quick and cheat. After you quick glimpse, flip the summary back over and try to complete more.

4. Once you've written a copy of the summary from (mostly) memory, use the summary to do another three minutes trying to memorize the annotated code. Simply read a part of the summary, and then look at the relevant part of the code and try to remember it. You could even do just three minutes per little function.

5. Once you've spent time attempting to remember the annotated code, flip *that* over and using the summary try to recall the code on your notepad. Again, when you get stuck, flip the annotation over quick and cheat.

6. Keep doing this until you can do an alright copy of the code on paper. Your paper code doesn't have to be perfect Python but should be pretty close to the original code.

It may seem like this is going to be impossible but you'd be surprised how much you can remember when you do this. You'll also be surprised at how well you understand the *concept* of a dictionary once you're done doing this. This isn't simple rote memorization but rather building a concept map that you can actually use when you attempt to implement the `Dictionary` yourself.

WARNING! If you are the kind of person who has anxiety about memorizing anything, then this exercise will be a *huge* help for you in the future. Being able to follow a procedure to memorize something helps overcome any frustration at memorizing a topic. Rather than flounder around "failing" at it, you get to watch slow improvement over a consistent process. As you do this, you'll see ways and hacks to improve your recall and do it better. You'll just have to trust me that this seems like a slow way to learn something, but it ends up being much faster than other techniques.

Implement from Memory

It is now time to walk to your computer—leaving your paper notes in another room or on the floor—and attempt your first implementation from memory. Your first attempt may be a complete disaster, but that's totally alright. You most likely aren't used to trying to implement anything from memory. Just put down anything you remember, and when you get to the end of your thread, walk back into the other room and do some more memorization. After a few trips to your memory room you'll get into it and the memories will flow better. It's alright to need to visit your memory notes over and over. It's all about *trying* to retain the memories of the code and improve your skills.

I recommend that you write whatever comes to your mind first, whether that's a test, code, or both. Then use what you can recall to implement or recall other parts of the code. If you sit down and remember the `test_set` function name and a few lines of code, then write those down. Take advantage of them being in your mind right away. Once you have that, use this test to remember or implement the `Dictionary.set` function as best you can. Your goal is to use any information you can to build and implement other information.

You should also try to use your *understanding* of the `Dictionary` to implement the code. Don't simply try to have photographic recall of each line. That's actually impossible as nobody has photographic memory (look it up, nobody does). What most people have is an okay memory that triggers conceptual understandings they can use. You should do the same thing and use what you *know* of how a `Dictionary` works to create your own copy. In the example above, you know that a `Dictionary.set` functions a certain way, and you'll need a way to get the slots and buckets ... so that means you need `get_slot` and `get_bucket`. You aren't photographically memorizing each character; you're remembering all the key concepts and using them.

Repeat

The *most* important part of this exercise is that there is no failure in having to repeat this process a few times to get better at it. You'll do this for the rest of these data structures in the book, so you'll get plenty of practice. If you have to go back and memorize 100 times that's alright. Eventually you'll only need to do 50, and then the next time only 10, and then eventually you'll be able to implement a `Dictionary` from memory easily. Just keep attempting it, and try to approach it like a meditation so you can relax while you do it.

Study Drills

1. My tests are very limited. Write a more extensive test.

2. How would the sorting algorithms from Exercise 16 help this data structure?

3. What happens when you randomize the keys and values to this data structure? Does a sorting algorithm help?

4. What impact does `num_buckets` have on the data structure?

Break It

Your brain may be fried, but take a break, and then try to break this code. This implementation is *easily* thrashed and overwhelmed with data. How about strange edge cases? Can you add *anything* as a key or only strings? What will cause problems? Finally, can you do any sneaky tricks to the code to make it seem like it works fine, but it's actually broken in some clever way?

Measuring Performance

In this exercise you're going to learn to use several tools to analyze the performance of the data structures and algorithms you've created. To keep this introduction focused and small we'll look at the performance of the `sorting.py` algorithms from Exercise 16, and then in the video I'll analyze the performance of all the data structures we've done so far.

Performance analysis and tuning is one of my favorite activities in computer programming. I'm that guy who will sit with a ball of tangled yarn while I watch TV and just pick it apart until it's all nice and orderly. I love teasing apart complicated mysteries, and code performance is one of the best complicated mysteries. There are also nice, useful tools for analyzing the performance of code, which makes it much nicer than debugging by comparison.

When you're coding don't try to implement performance improvements unless they're obvious. I much prefer to keep the initial version of my code very simple and naïve so that I can ensure it works correctly. Then once it's working well, but maybe slow, I break out my profiling tools and start to look for ways to make it faster *without reducing the stability*. This last part is key because many programmers feel it's alright to reduce the stability and safety of their code if that makes the code faster.

The Tools

In this exercise we'll be covering many different tools that are useful for Python and some general strategies for improving the performance of any code. The tools we'll use are

- `timeit` (https://docs.python.org/3/library/timeit.html)
- `cProfile` and `profile` (https://docs.python.org/2/library/profile.html)

Make sure you install any that need to be installed before you continue. Then get your copy of the `sorting.py` and `test_sorting.py` files so we can apply each of these tools to those algorithms.

timeit

The `timeit` module isn't very useful. All it does is take a *string* of Python code and run it with some timing. You can't pass it function references, `.py` files, or anything other than a string. We can test how long the `test_bubble_sort` function takes by writing this at the end of `test_sorting.py`:

```
if __name__ == '__main__':
    import timeit
    print(timeit.timeit("test_bubble_sort()",
        setup="from __main__ import test_bubble_sort"))
```

It also doesn't produce useful measurements or any information on *why* something might be slow. We need a way to measure how long pieces of code take to run, and this is simply too clunky to be useful.

cProfile and profile

The next two tools are *much* more useful for measuring the performance of your code. I recommend using cProfile to analyze your code's running time, and save profile for when you need more flexibility in your analysis. To run cProfile against your test, change the bottom of the test_sorting.py file to simply run the test functions:

```
if __name__ == '__main__':
    test_bubble_sort()
    test_merge_sort()
```

And change the max_numbers to around 800 or a big enough number that you can measure an effect. Once you do that then run cProfile on your code:

```
$ python -m cProfile -s cumtime test_sorting.py | grep sorting.py
```

I'm using | grep sorting.py just to narrow the output to the files I care about, but drop that part of the command to see the full output. The results I get on my fairly fast computer for 800 numbers is:

```
  ncalls  tottime  percall  cumtime  percall filename:lineno(function)
       1    0.000    0.000    0.145    0.145 test_sorting.py:1(<module>)
       1    0.000    0.000    0.128    0.128 test_sorting.py:25 \
                                             (test_bubble_sort)
       1    0.125    0.125    0.125    0.125 sorting.py:6(bubble_sort)
       1    0.000    0.000    0.009    0.009 sorting.py:1(<module>)
       1    0.000    0.000    0.008    0.008 test_sorting.py:33 \
                                             (test_merge_sort)
       2    0.001    0.000    0.006    0.003 test_sorting.py:7(random_list)
       1    0.000    0.000    0.005    0.005 sorting.py:37(merge_sort)
  1599/1    0.001    0.000    0.005    0.005 sorting.py:47(merge_node)
7500/799    0.004    0.000    0.004    0.000 sorting.py:72(merge)
     799    0.001    0.000    0.001    0.000 sorting.py:27(count)
       2    0.000    0.000    0.000    0.000 test_sorting.py:14(is_sorted)
```

I've added the headers back to the top so you can see what this output means. Each header means the following

ncalls   Number of calls to this function

tottime   Total execution time

percall   Total time per call to the function

cumtime   Cumulative time for this function

percall   Cumulative time per call

filename:lineno(function)   The filename, line number, and function involved

Those header names are also the options available for the -s parameter. We can then do a quick analysis of this output:

- `bubble_sort` is called once, but `merge_node` is called a 1599 times, and `merge` even more at 7500 calls. This is because `merge_node` and `merge` are recursive, so they'll produce a large number of calls sorting a random list of 800 elements.

- Even though `bubble_sort` isn't called nearly as much as `merge` or `merge_node`, it is a *lot* slower. This fits with the performance expectations of the two algorithms. The worst case for merge sort is O(n log n), but for bubble sort it's O(n^2). If you have 800 elements then 800 log 800 is about 5347, while 800^2 is 640000! These numbers don't necessarily translate into exact seconds these algorithms run, but they do translate into a relative comparison.

- The `count` function is called 799 times, which is most likely a huge waste. Our implementation of the `DoubleLinkedList` doesn't track the count of elements and instead has to run through the list every single time you want to know a count. We use that same method in the `count` function here, and that leads to 799 runs through the whole list for 800 elements. Change the `max_numbers` to 600 or 500 to see a pattern here. Notice how `count` is run n-1 times in our implementation? That means we go through almost all 800 elements.

Next let's look at how the `dllist.py` numbers impact this performance too:

```
$ python —m cProfile —s cumtime test_sorting.py | grep dllist.py
   ncalls  tottime  percall  cumtime  percall filename:lineno(function)
   1200    0.000    0.000    0.001    0.000 dllist.py:66(shift)
   1200    0.001    0.000    0.001    0.000 dllist.py:19(push)
   1200    0.000    0.000    0.000    0.000 dllist.py:3(__init__)
      1    0.000    0.000    0.000    0.000 dllist.py:1(<module>)
      1    0.000    0.000    0.000    0.000 dllist.py:1(DoubleLinkedListNode)
      2    0.000    0.000    0.000    0.000 dllist.py:15(__init__)
      1    0.000    0.000    0.000    0.000 dllist.py:13(DoubleLinkedList)
```

Again I've added the headers back so you can see what's going on. In this you can see that the `dllist.py` functions don't impact performance that much compared to the `merge`, `merge_node`, and `count` functions. This is important because most programmers would run to optimize the `DoubleLinkedList` data structure where there's bigger gains to be made with the `merge_sort` implementation and completely ditch the `bubble_sort`. Always start with where you can get the most improvement for the least effort.

Analyzing Performance

Analyzing performance is simply a matter of finding out what is slow and then trying to determine why it's slow. It's similar to debugging, except you are trying your best not to change the behavior of the code.

When you're done, the code should work exactly the same but just do it faster. There are times when fixing the performance also finds bugs, but it's best to not attempt complete redesigns when you're trying to speed it up. One thing at a time.

Another important thing to have before you start analyzing performance is some metric of what is *needed* of the software. Fast is generally always good, but without a target you'll end up proposing possible solutions that are completely unnecessary. If your system is performing at 50 requests/second and you really only need 100 requests/second, then there's no point proposing a complete rewrite in Haskell to get 200. This process is all about "most money saved for the least effort possible," and you need some kind of measurement to target.

You can get most of these measurements from your operations staff, and they should have good graphs showing CPU usage, requests/second being served, frame rates, and whatever they feel is important or that customers say is important. You can then work with them to devise tests that demonstrate the slowness that needs to be targeted so you can improve the code to reach the goals they need. You may be able to squeeze more performance out of the system, saving money. You may attempt it and come to the conclusion that it's just a hard problem requiring more CPU resources. With a metric to target, you'll have an idea of when to give up or that you've done enough.

The simplest process you can use to analyze performance is the following:

1. Run a performance analyzer on the code as I've done here using your tests. The more information you can get, the better. See the *Further Study* section for additional tools that are free. Ask around for other tools people may be using to analyze the speed of the system.

2. Identify the *slowest* and *smallest* pieces of code. Don't go to a giant function and try to analyze it. Many times these functions are slow because they are using a bunch of other slow functions. In finding the slowest and smallest first you're more likely to get the most gains for the least effort.

3. Do a code review of these slow pieces of code and anything they touch, looking for possible reasons the code is slow. Do you have loops inside loops? Calling a function too often? Look for simple things that are possible to change *before* investigating complex techniques like caching.

4. Once you have a list of all the slowest smallest functions and simple changes to make them faster, look for patterns. Are you doing this anywhere else you can't see?

5. Finally, look for possible big improvements you can make if there's no simple changes to small functions you can make. Maybe it truly is time for a complete rewrite? Don't do this until you've at least *attempted* the simple fixes first.

6. Keep a list of all the things you tried and all the performance gains you made. If you don't, then you'll constantly come back to functions you already worked on and waste effort.

As you work this process the idea of "slowest and smallest" will change. You'll fix a dozen 10-line functions and make them faster, which means now you can look at that 100-line function that's now the slowest. Once you have that 100-line function running quicker, you can look at the larger groups of functions being run and come up with strategies to speed them up.

Finally, the best way to speed anything up is to not do it at all. If you're doing multiple checks of the same condition, find a way to avoid doing it more than once. If you're calculating the same column in a database repeatedly, do it once. If you call a function in a tight loop, but the data rarely changes, check out memoization or pre-calculate a table. In many cases you can trade storage for computation by simply calculating things ahead of time and storing them once.

In the next exercise we'll actually go through improving the performance of these algorithms using this process.

Exercise Challenge

Your challenge for this exercise is to apply what I did with the `bubble_sort` and `merge_sort` to all the data structures and algorithms you've created so far. You aren't expected to improve them yet but to just take notes and analyze the performance while developing tests that demonstrate performance problems. Resist the temptation to fix anything right now because we'll be *improving* the performance in Exercise 19.

Study Drills

1. Run these profiling tools on all of your code so far and analyze the performance.
2. Compare your results to the theoretical results for the algorithms and data structures.

Breaking It

Try to write pathological tests that cause the data structures to break down. You may need to feed them large amounts of data, but use the profiling information to make sure you're doing it right.

Further Study

1. Look at line_profiler (https://github.com/rkern/line_profiler) as another performance measurement tool. Its advantage is you can measure only the functions you care about, but the disadvantage is you have to change your source to do it.
2. pyprof2calltree (https://pypi.python.org/pypi/pyprof2calltree) and KCacheGrind (https://kcachegrind.github.io/html/Home.html) are more advanced tools but really only work on Linux. In the video I demonstrate using them under Linux.

Improving Performance

This is a mostly video exercise where I will demonstrate *improving* the performance of the code you've written so far, but first you should attempt it. You've analyzed how slow and fast the code is from Exercise 18, so now it's time to implement some of your ideas. I'll give you a quick list of things to look for and change when fixing simple performance problems:

1. Loops inside loops repeating calculations that can be avoided. The bubble sort is the classic case of this, and that's why I taught it. Once you can see how terrible bubble sort is compared to other methods you'll start to recognize this as a common pattern to avoid.

2. Repeatedly calculating something that doesn't really change or can be calculated once during the change. The use of a `count()` function in the `sorting.py` and other data structures is a great example of this. You can keep track of the count inside the functions to the data structure. Every time you add, you can increase it and every time you remove, decrease it. There's no need to go through the whole list every time. You can also use this pre-calculated count to improve the logic of other functions by checking for `count == 0`.

3. Using the wrong data structure for the job. In the `Dictionary` I'm using the `DoubleLinkedList` as a demonstration of this problem. A `Dictionary` needs to have random access to element, at least in the list of buckets. Using a `DoubleLinkedList` with `DoubleLinkedList` inside means every time you want to access the *n*th element you have to go through all elements up to *n*. Replacing this with a Python list would vastly improve the performance. This was an exercise in using your existing code to craft a data structure from simpler data structures so not necessarily an exercise in making the best Python `Dictionary` (it already has one).

4. Using the wrong algorithms on data structures. Bubble sort is obviously the wrong algorithm (never use that again), but remember how merge sort and quick sort are better, depending on the data structure? Merge sort is great for these kinds of linked data structures but not as good on arrays like Python's `list`. Quick sort is better on a `list` but not really as good on linked data structures.

5. Not optimizing for common operations in the best place. In the `DoubleLinkedList` you'll frequently start at the beginning of a bucket and search the slots for a value. In the current code these slots are simply added as they come in, and that may be random or not. If you adopted a discipline of *sorting* these lists on insert, then finding an element would be easier and quicker. You could stop when a slot's value is greater than what you're looking for because you know it's already sorted. Doing this makes *inserts* slower but speeds up nearly every other operation, so choose the right design for the job. If you have a need to do tons of inserts, then this isn't smart. But if your analysis shows you're doing few inserts but many accesses, then this is a way to speed it up.

6. Hand rolling your own instead of using existing code. We're doing exercises to learn data structures, but in the real world you would not do this. Python already has great data structures that are built into the language and optimized. You *should* use those first, and *if* a performance analysis says your own data structure would be quicker *then* write your own. Even then you should look up an existing data structure someone else has already proven works instead of rolling your own. In this exercise, write a few tests that compare your `Dictionary` and lists to the Python built-in types to see how far off you may be by comparison.

7. Using recursion in a language that's not good at it. The `merge_sort` code can be broken by simply handing it a list that's bigger than the Python stack. Try giving it something insane like 3000 elements and then slowly bring that down till you find the sweet spot that causes Python to run out of stack. Python doesn't do certain recursive optimizations, so using recursion without special considerations is going to fail like this. In this case, rewriting the `merge_sort` to use a loop would be better (but much more difficult).

These are some of the big wins you should have discovered during the analysis in Exercise 18. Your task now is to attempt to implement them and improve the performance of this code.

Exercise Challenge

Attempt to use your analysis and the description of suggested improvements above to methodically improve the performance of your code. Methodically means to do it in a lock step controlled way using *data* to confirm that you have actually improved things. Here's your process to follow during this exercise:

1. Pick your first, smallest, slowest piece of code and make sure there's a test showing how slow it is. Make sure you have a series of measurements that give you an idea of the speed. Graph it if you can.

2. Attempt your speed improvement changes and then run your test again. Keep trying to squeeze all the performance you can out of this piece of code.

3. If you attempt a code change and it does *not* improve things, then either figure out what you did wrong or back out that change and try something else. This is important because you are working on a hypothesis, so if you leave a useless code change in it may change the performance of other functions you can fix. Back the change out and try a different approach or move on to another piece of code.

4. Re-run your measurements of the *other* smallest slowest pieces of code to see if they have changed. Your fixes may have fixed other code, so reconfirm what you think you know.

5. Once you've gone through everything you've identified, run your measurements again and pick new pieces of code to attempt to improve.

6. Keep your tests from step 1 (they should be automated tests) because you want to avoid regressions. If you see a change to a function causing other functions to be slower, then either fix that or simply back that change out and try a new approach.

Further Study

You should study the Python Timsort original email (https://mail.python.org/pipermail/python-dev/2002-July/026837.html) and finally the bug found in 2015 (http://bugs.python.org/issue23515) by researchers from the EU FP7 ENVISAGE (http://envisage-project.eu/proving-android-java-and-python-sorting-algorithm-is-broken-and-how-to-fix-it/). The original email was sent in 2002 and subsequently implemented. It took 13 *years* before this bug was found. Keep that in mind when you go to implement your own ideas for algorithms. Even top-notch developers on big projects have lurking bugs in their algorithms that aren't found for a very long time. Another example would be the OpenSSL project, which had lurking bugs for decades simply because everyone believed that "professional cryptographers" created the code. Turns out, even supposedly professional cryptographers can write terrible code. Getting new algorithms correct requires special skills and—I think—the use of a theorem-proving tool to validate the correctness. Unless you have this background, creating new algorithms and data structures can lead to your peril. That includes cryptography algorithms and encrypted network protocols. Implementing algorithms other people have proven is totally fine and a good exercise, so long as you are up front about your skills in implementation. But don't go crafting your own hair-brained data structures without some help.

Binary Search Trees

In this exercise I'm going to teach you to translate an English description of a data structure into working code. You already know how to analyze the code for an algorithm or data structure using the master copy method. You also know how to read a p-code (psuedo-code) description of an algorithm. Now you will combine the two and learn how to break down a rather loose English description of the binary search tree.

I'm going to start off right away and warn you to *not* visit the Wikipedia page when you do this exercise. The binary search tree description on Wikipedia has mostly working Python code for the data structure, so it would defeat the point of this exercise. If you get stuck then you'll be able to read any resources you can, but first try to do it from just my descriptions here.

BSTree Requirements

In Exercise 16 you saw how a merge sort takes a flat, linked list and seems to convert it into a tree of sorted parts. It keeps cutting the list into smaller pieces and then assembles the pieces back together by sorting lesser valued parts on the "left" and greater valued parts on the right. In a way, a binary search tree (BSTree) is a data structure that does this sorting right away and never tries to keep the items in a list. The main usage for a BSTree is to use a tree to organize pairs of key=value nodes in order *ahead* of time, as you insert or delete them.

A BSTree does this by starting the tree at a root key=value, and having a right or left path (link). If you insert a new key=value, then the BSTree's job is to start at the root and compare the key to each node: going left if your new key is less-than and going right if your key is greater-than-equal. Eventually the BSTree finds a position in the tree that—should you follow the original path—will find it by following the same process. All operations after that do the same thing by comparing any keys to each node, moving left and right until it either finds the node or reaches a dead end.

In this way a BSTree is an alternative to a Dictionary from Exercise 17, and so it should have the same operations. The basic BSTreeNode would need left, right, key, and value attributes to create the tree structure. You may also need a parent attribute depending on how you do this. The BSTree then needs the following operations on a root BSTreeNode:

get   Given a key, walk the tree to find the node, or return None if you reach a dead end. You go left if the given key is less-than the node's key. You go right if the key is greater-than the node's key. If you read a node with no left or right, then you're done and the node does not exist. There is a way to do this using recursion and using a while loop.

set   This is nearly the same as get except once you reach that dead-end node you simply attach a new BSTreeNode on the left or right, thus extending the tree down one more branch.

delete   Deleting nodes from a BSTree is a complex operation, so I have a whole section just on delete. The short version is you have three conditions: the node is a leaf (no children), has one child, or has two children. If it's a leaf then just remove it. If it has one child, then replace it with the child. If it has two children, then it gets really complicated so read the section on deleting below.

list   Walk the tree and print everything out. The important piece to list is that you can walk the tree in different ways to produce different output. If you walk the left, then the right paths, you get something different than if you do the inverse. If you go all the way to the bottom and then print as you come up the tree toward root, you get yet another kind of output. You can also print the nodes as you go down the tree, from root to the "leaves." Try different styles to see which one does what.

Deleting

Remember we have three conditions to deal with when deleting a node (which I'll call D):

1.   The D node is a "leaf" node because it has no children (not left or right). Just remove it from the parent.

2.   The D node has only one child (either left or right but not both). In that case you can simply move the value of this child to the D node, then delete the child. That effectively replaces the D node with the child (or, "moves the child up").

3.   The D node has both a left and a right child, which means it's time to do some major surgery. First, find the minimum child of the D.right node called the successor. Set the D.key to the successor.key, and then do the same delete on this successor's children using its key.

You will most likely also need an operation for find_minimum and for replace_node_in_parent to perform those two operations. I mention that you *might* need a parent attribute depending on how you implement it. I'd say go with a parent node as that's easier in most cases.

WARNING! Everyone hates deleting from a tree. It's a complicated operation and even my favorite reference, *The Algorithm Design Manual, Second Edition,* by Steven S. Skiena (Springer, 2008), skips over it because the the implementation "looks a little ghastly." Don't be discouraged if you have a hard time figuring delete out.

Exercise Challenge

You are to implement your BSTree using this purposefully vague description. Try not to look at too many references while you make a first attempt, then when you get stuck go read how others have done it. The point of this exercise is to attempt to solve a complicated problem from an admittedly terrible description of it.

The trick to solving this is to first translate the paragraphs of English into rough p-code. Then translate the rough p-code to more exact p-code. Once you have a more exact p-code you can then translate that into Python. Pay special attention to specific words as a single word in English could mean a great many things in Python. Sometimes you just have to make a guess and run your tests to see if that's probably the right one.

Tests will also be very important, and it might be a good idea to apply the "test first" method to this problem. You know what each of these operations should do, so you can write a test for it, then make the test work.

Study Drills

1. Can you develop a pathological test that does inserts in such a way as to make the BSTree be nothing more than a fancy linked list?

2. What happens when you try to delete from this "pole" of a BSTree?

3. How does the speed of the BSTree compare to the speed of your newly optimized Dictionary?

4. How fast can you make the BSTree using your performance analysis and tuning process?

Binary Search

The binary search algorithm is a simple way to find an item in an already sorted list of items. It's easily described as taking a sorted list and continually partitioning it into halves until you either find it or you run out. If you did the complete Exercise 20, then this exercise should be relatively easy.

If we wanted to find a number X in an already sorted list of numbers we would do this:

1. Get the number in the middle of the list (M) and compare it to X.

2. If X == M, you're done.

3. If X > M, then find the middle of M+1 to the end of the list.

4. If X < M, then find the middle of M-1 to the beginning of the list.

5. Repeat, until either you find X or you have only 1 element left.

This works for anything that you can compare with equality. It will work on strings, numbers, and anything else you can order consistently.

Exercise Challenge

Your BSTree should already be doing a get operation that's similar to the binary search. The difference is the BSTree is already partitioned, so there's no need to do any more. In this exercise you'll implement the binary search for the DoubleLinkedList, Python's list, and compare those to the BSTree.get performance. Your goal is to learn the following:

1. How well does the BSTree compare to Python's list for simply finding some items?

2. How poorly does binary search work with DoubleLinkedList?

3. Do your pathological cases for BSTree also cause problems for a binary search on list?

When analyzing the performance, don't include the time it takes to sort the numbers. That's important when doing a global optimization, but in this case you only care about how fast the binary search works. You can also use Python's built-in list sorting algorithms to sort your list since that's not the point. This exercise is all about how fast search is between the three data structures.

Study Drills

1. Find out what the maximum number of possible comparisons is that this algorithm needs to make. Try to figure it out on your own first, and then research the algorithm to find out what the real answer is. After that just memorize the real answer.

2. Can any of your optimizations here be applied to the sorting algorithms?

3. Try to visualize what this algorithm is doing in each data structure. For example, in the `DoubleLinkedList` you can almost think of it as walking back and forth until it finds the answer.

4. To give yourself an extra challenge, try to make the `DoubleLinkedList` into a sorted linked list where every insert is always at the sorted position. Now write your performance analysis to *include* adding elements and sorting the lists of numbers to see how that improves total performance.

Further Study

Research other search algorithms, especially for strings. Many of these will be difficult to implement in Python because of the way Python's strings are implemented, but give it a try anyway.

Suffix Arrays

I 'd like to tell you a story about suffix arrays. I was interviewing at a company in Seattle during a time I was curious about how to most efficiently create a diff on an executable binary. My research brought me to the algorithms suffix array and suffix tree. The suffix array is simply where you sort all the suffixes of a string into a sorted list. The suffix tree is similar but done more like a BSTree than a list. These algorithms were fairly simple and had fast performance once you did the sorting operation. The problem they solved was finding the longest common substring between two strings (or in this case, lists of bytes).

You can make a suffix array in Python really easily:

Exercise 22 Python Session

```
1    >>> magic = "abracadabra"
2    >>> magic_sa = []
3    >>> for i in range(0, len(magic)):
4    ...        magic_sa.append(magic[i:])
5    ...
6    >>> magic_sa
7    ['abracadabra', 'bracadabra', 'racadabra', 'acadabra',
8     'cadabra', 'adabra', 'dabra', 'abra', 'bra', 'ra', 'a']
9    >>> magic_sa = sorted(magic_sa)
10   >>> magic_sa
11   ['a', 'abra', 'abracadabra', 'acadabra', 'adabra', 'bra',
12    'bracadabra', 'cadabra', 'dabra', 'ra', 'racadabra']
13   >>>
```

As you can see, I simply took the suffixes of the string in order, and then sorted the list. But, what does this do for me? Once I have this list, then I can find any suffix I want by simply doing a *binary search on this list*. This example is very crude, but in real code you can do this very quickly, and you can keep track of all the original indexes so you can then reference the suffixes' original locations. It is very fast compared to other search algorithms and very useful in things like DNA analysis.

Back to the interview in Seattle. I'm in this cold room being interviewed by C++ programmers for a Java job. As you can tell this isn't a very fun interview, and I definitely don't think I'll get the job. I hadn't written any C++ in many years and the job was for Java, of which I was an expert at the time. In walks the next interviewer and he asks me, "How would you find a substring in a string."

Great! I've been studying the hell out of this problem in my free time. I'll nail it! I jump up and walk up to the whiteboard and explain to the guy how to make a suffix tree, how it improves search performance, how a modified heap sort makes it faster, how a suffix tree works, why it's better than a ternary search tree, and how to do it in C. I figure, if I can show how to write one in C then that'll demonstrate I'm not just a Java dude with no hardcore metal background.

The guy is stunned. Like I opened a bag of fresh durian in the interview room. He looks at the board, and stammers, "Uh, uh, I was kind of looking for something about the Boyer-Moore search algorithm? Do you know that?" I screw up my face a little and say, "Yeah but, like 10 years ago." He shakes his head, grabs his stuff, and gets up saying, "Alright, well I'll let everyone know what I think."

A few minutes later in walks the next interviewer. He looks up at the white board, chuckles and scoffs at me, then asks me another C++ template meta-programming question that I couldn't answer. I did not get the job.

Exercise Challenge

In this exercise you're going to take my little Python session and create your own suffix array search class. This class will take a string, carve it into a list of suffixes, and then allow the following operations on it:

find_shortest   Find the shortest substring that has this beginning. In the example above, if I search for "abra" then it should return "abra," not "abracadabra".

find_longest   Find the longest substring that has this beginning. If I search for "abra" it should return "abracadabra".

find_all   Find all substrings that start with this beginning. This means "abra" returns both "abra" and "abracadabra."

You'll want to have a good automated test for this, plus have some performance measurements. We'll be using those in later exercises. Once you are done you'll want to do the *Study Drills* to complete this exercise.

Study Drills

1.   Once you have your tests working, rewrite this to use your BSTree to do the suffix sorting and searching. You can also use the value of each BSTreeNode to keep track of where this substring exists in the original string. You can then keep the original string around.

2.   How does the BStree change your code for the different searching operations? Does it make it simpler or harder?

Further Study

Definitely research suffix arrays and their applications. They are incredibly useful but not too well known by most programmers.

Ternary Search Trees

The final data structure we'll investigate is called a ternary search tree (TSTree), and it's useful for quickly finding a string in a set of strings. It's similar to a BSTree but instead of two children it has three children, and each child is only a single character rather than an entire string. In the BSTree you had a left and right child for the "less-than" and "greater-than-equal" branches of the tree. With a TSTree you have left, middle, and right branches for "less-than," "equal-to," and "greater-than" branches. This lets you take a string, break it into characters, and then walk the TSTree one character at a time until you find it or you run out.

The TSTree is effectively trading space for speed by breaking the set of possible keys you need to search into one character nodes. Each of these nodes will take up more space than the same keys in a BSTree, but this enables you to find keys by *only* comparing the characters in the key you want. With a BSTree you have to compare most of the characters in both the search key and node key once each node. With a TSTree you only compare each letter of the search key, and when you get to the end that's it.

The other thing that a TSTree is very good for is knowing when a key does *not* exist in the set. Imagine you have a key that's 10 characters long and you need to find it in a set of other keys, but you need to stop fast if the key does not exist. With a TSTree you could stop at one or two characters, reach the end of the tree, and know this key does not exist. You'll at most compare only 10 characters in the key to find this out, which is much fewer character comparisons than a BSTree would make. A BSTree could compare all the characters in a 10 character key once for every single node in the most pathological case (where the BSTree is basically a linked list) before deciding the key does not exist.

Exercise Challenge

In this exercise you're going to partially do another master copy and then complete the TSTree on your own. The code you'll need is the following:

tstree.py

```
1    class TSTreeNode(object):
2
3        def __init__(self, key, value, low, eq, high):
4            self.key = key
5            self.low = low
6            self.eq = eq
7            self.high = high
8            self.value = value
9
10
11   class TSTree(object):
12
```

```
13          def __init__(self):
14              self.root = None
15
16          def _get(self, node, keys):
17              key = keys[0]
18              if key < node.key:
19                  return self._get(node.low, keys)
20              elif key == node.key:
21                  if len(keys) > 1:
22                      return self._get(node.eq, keys[1:])
23                  else:
24                      return node.value
25              else:
26                  return self._get(node.high, keys)
27
28          def get(self, key):
29              keys = [x for x in key]
30              return self._get(self.root, keys)
31
32          def _set(self, node, keys, value):
33              next_key = keys[0]
34
35              if not node:
36                  # what happens if you add the value here?
37                  node = TSTreeNode(next_key, None, None, None, None)
38
39              if next_key < node.key:
40                  node.low = self._set(node.low, keys, value)
41              elif next_key == node.key:
42                  if len(keys) > 1:
43                      node.eq = self._set(node.eq, keys[1:], value)
44                  else:
45                      # what happens if you DO NOT add the value here?
46                      node.value = value
47              else:
48                  node.high = self._set(node.high, keys, value)
49
50              return node
51
52          def set(self, key, value):
53              keys = [x for x in key]
54              self.root = self._set(self.root, keys, value)
```

You'll need to study this using the master copy method you learned. Pay special attention to how the node.eq path is handled and how the node.value is set. Once you have an understanding of how get and set work, you'll then implement the remaining functions and all the tests. The functions to implement are

> **find_shortest**   Given a key K, find the shortest key/value pair that starts with K. This means if you have "apple" and "application" in your set, then a call to find_shortest("appl") will return "apple" and the value associated with it.

find_longest   Given a key K, find the longest key/value pair that starts with K. Using the example of "apple" and "application," a call to `find_longest("appl")` would return "application" and the value associated with it.

find_all   Given a key K, find *all* of the key/value pairs that start with K. I would implement this first, and then base `find_shortest` and `find_longest` on that.

find_part   Given a key K, find the shortest key that has at least a part of the beginning of K. Investigate how where you set the `node.value` makes this work.

Study Drills

1. Look at the comments in the original code regarding where you place the `value` during `_set`. Does changing this change the meaning of `get`, and why or why not?

2. Make sure you thrash this with randomness and create some performance measurements.

3. You can also do partial matching matching in a `TSTree`. I consider this extra credit, so try to implement these and see what you come up with. Partial matching is where you match `"a.p.e"` on `"apple"`, `"anpxe"`, and `"ajpqe"`.

4. How can you search for endings of strings? Hint: Don't over think this.

Fast URL Search

We will end the section on data structures and algorithms with a performance measurement challenge that applies your data structures to an actual problem. I've written a few web servers in my time, and one problem that constantly comes up is matching URL paths to "actions." You'll find this problem in every web framework, web server, and anything that has to "route" information based on a key that is hierarchical. When your web server receives the URL /do/this/stuff/, it has to figure out if each part is possibly attached to some kind of action or configuration. If you configured a web application at /do/, then what should your web server do with /this/stuff/? Should it consider that a failure or pass it to the web application? What if there's a directory at /do/this/? And, how do you detect bad URLs quickly so you're not processing giant requests that don't exist?

This kind of hierarchical search comes up frequently enough that it's a good final test of your ability to apply algorithms and data structures to problems as well as a test of your ability to do performance analysis.

Exercise Challenge

First, be sure you understand what a URL is and how they are used. If you don't, then I suggest you take the time to go write *one* small Flask application that has some complex routing in it. It's this routing that you'll be implementing.

Next, you are expected to do the following:

1. Create a simple base URLRouter class that you'll subclass for all your implementations. You should be able to do the following to this URLRouter:

    a. Add a new URL with an associated object.

    b. Get an exact match of a URL. A search for /do/this/stuff/ returns only what's at exactly that.

    c. Get the best match for a URL. A search for /do/this/stuff/ will match /do/ if that's the only match there is.

    d. Get all the objects that start with this URL.

    e. Get the shortest URL matching object. A search for /do/this/stuff/ would return /do/ but not /do/this/.

    f. Get the longest URL matching object. A search for /do/this/stuff/ would return /do/this/ but not /do/.

2. Create and test a subclass of the URLRouter using the TSTree as this will be the easiest to do. Be sure to test the following:

    a. Randomized URLs and paths of different lengths in both the TSTree and what you search for

    b. Finding only partial paths in the different situations

    c. Completely non-existent paths

    d. Really long paths that exist and don't exist

3. Once you have this subclass working and tested, generalize your test so you can run it on all the implementations you're going to make.

4. Then, attempt implementations that use DoubleLinkedList, BSTree, Dictionary, and Python's dict. Make sure your generalized test works for all of these.

5. Once you have that, start analyzing the performance of each of these implementations for the different operations.

The goal is to see how fast a TSTree is compared to other data structures. It might beat most of them, but maybe the Python dict will win most of the time because it is optimized for Python. You may even want to make a bet as to which data structure will have the best performance for each operation.

Study Drills

1. I left out the SuffixArray because it is similar to the TSTree, but to use it for this you'll have to add the same operations. Do that and then see how SuffixArray compares.

2. Research how your favorite web server or web framework does this. You'll find not many people working with URLs know what a ternary search tree is despite how useful it is for this common operation.

Further Study

I highly recommend the book *The Algorithm Design Manual, Second Edition,* by Steven S. Skiena (Springer, 2008) if you want to dive deeper into algorithms and data structures. His book uses C, so you may need to read *Learn C the Hard Way* first to be able to go through it. Other than that it's a very good book as it covers the theory, but also the practical aspects, of implementing and analyzing the performance of algorithms and data structures.

PART IV
Intermediate Projects

In Part III you learned the basics of data structures and algorithms, but more importantly you learned to audit and test code. You didn't audit and test your *own* code. You just reviewed mine for defects or deficiencies in ways I dictated to you. The goal of Part IV is to now turn that auditing eye on your *own* code with a set of challenge mode projects. Your job during these next five projects is the following:

1. Conduct a 45-minute hacking session to create the project and get going.

2. Audit this first hack using what you learned in Part III to find potential defects and problems in your implementation.

3. Proceed to clean up and develop your hack into something official for another 45 minutes.

4. Audit that 45-minute session to refine it.

The only difference between these 45-minute sessions and your first batch of projects is you don't need to be as strict about the time. The 45 minutes is only a guide to make sure you don't go too long before reviewing your code. There's no point in reviewing code that is stopped in the middle of a good idea or implementation. Obviously code that's half done isn't going to be reviewed very well. The key is to work for about 45 minutes, and when you hit a stopping point *then* review what you've done.

During this section you are to refer back to the checklist from Part III and follow it very strictly. It's good to take a 10–15 minute break before you conduct an audit so that you clear your head and can switch into the critical mode of thinking.

As you work on these projects I will suggest algorithms that you can use in the project when they apply. You don't have to use the algorithms you implemented, but you should try, just to see how they work. Chances are they are *not* better than Python's existing data structures (`lists` and `dicts`) as Python's data structures have been highly tuned to be as fast as possible. It's still a good exercise to try to use algorithms so that you learn when to use them and how to check them.

Tracking Your Defects

Finally, you will be asked to *track* your defect rates. Just as you did when tracking your features complete in Part II, you will track how many defects you find in your audits and what kind of defects they are. Keep a log in your journal of what you find by creating a grid with the defect type across the top and the time of day on the left. You can also just graph the results directly if you want or use a spreadsheet. Your goal with tracking these defects found is to begin to find out what kind of mistakes you frequently make during your programming sessions so that you can attempt to prevent them or simply watch for them in audits.

xargs

We are returning to challenge mode exercises and to warm you up you'll be implementing `xargs`. This should be a straightforward implementation for you, but `xargs` can be complex as you'll need to launch *other* programs to make it work. The Python module you'll want to investigate is `subprocess`, which can run other programs from Python and collect their output. You'll need to understand that module to complete `xargs` and many of the other projects later in the book, so study it well.

Exercise Challenge

Implement `xargs` for just 45 minutes so you can get something working that you can audit. Remember, this first hack is about getting the project going, not making something perfect. You'll use subsequent steps in this project to refine it and make it better. Remember that you can type

```
man xargs
```

to get the manual page for `xargs` and research how it works. It's a handy Unix tool, but you can also use `find` to do nearly the same thing. As you implement `xargs` try to find out what advantage it has over `find -exec`.

After your 45-minute hack you should take a break and then conduct an objective audit of the code using the checklist for auditing code described in Exercise 13. Don't fix the code, just write comments indicating what needs to change and what defects there are. It's difficult to remain objective while also trying to fix things, so just note problems in the audit and then fix them in the next round.

You will then conduct a squence of code/audit timed sessions to get used to the idea of doing audits. Take as long as you need to implement as much of `xargs` as you can, and then move on to the next project.

WARNING! Remember to track your defects in your journal so you can do run charts of them and look for trends.

Study Drills

1. During this process of code/audit did you find anything you continually get wrong? Write these down as potential things to work on.

2. Is there a particular point in your code/audit process that has more or fewer defects? Are there more in the beginning than after three or four? Why might this be?

3. Try writing automated tests for your implementation of xargs and see if that drops your defect rate. In the next exercise you will do a more controlled testing study like this, but give it a shot now to see what you find.

hexdump

Y ou've done a warmup with xargs and are now working in the cycle of code then audit. You are now going to try to complete the next challenge with a "test first" approach. This is where you write a test that describes your expected behavior, and then you implement the behavior until the test passes. You are going to be copying the hexdump utility and attempting to match your version's output to the real version's. This is where test first development really helps since it automates the process of mimicking another piece of software.

This technique is very useful when you need to write a replacement for a terrible piece of software. A common job in software is to work on a project that aims to replace an older system with a more modern implementation. An example is replacing an old COBOL banking system with a fresh, new, hot Django system. The motivation is typically to make it easier to maintain and extend by using something easier to work with than the old system. If you can write a set of automated tests that validate the behavior of the old system and then point that test suite at the new system, then you have a way to confirm that your replacement works ... mostly. Trust me, these replacement jobs are nearly impossible and don't succeed too often, but an automated test helps.

In this exercise you'll add to your process the following:

1.   Write a test case that runs the original hexdump in a scenario you need to implement. Let's say the -C option. You'll either need to use subprocess to launch it or simply run it ahead of time and save the results to a file that you load.

2.   Write the code that makes this test work by having the test run *your* version of hexdump and then compare the results. If they aren't equal, then you didn't do it right.

3.   Audit both the test code and your code.

I chose hexdump because the difficulty is in replicating its strange output format for viewing binary data. There's nothing too complicated about how it works. It's just matching the output that you need to get right. This helps you practice test first testing.

WARNING! When I say "write a test first," I do *not* mean a whole massive test.py file with all the functions and huge amounts of imaginary code. I mean what I've taught in the past. Write a little test case—maybe just one-tenth of one test function—then write the code to make that work, and then bounce back and forth between the two. The more you know about the code the more of the test *case* you can write, but don't write reams of test code with nothing to run against it. Work incrementally instead.

Exercise Challenge

The hexdump command is useful when you want to see the contents of a file that is not viewable text. It displays the bytes in a file in various useful formats, including hex, octal, and with an ASCII output trailing on the side. The difficulty in implementing your own hexdump isn't reading the data or even converting it to different formats. You can do that easily using the hex, oct, int, and ord functions in Python. The original format string operators are also useful as there are options for doing fixed precision octal and hex formatting.

The real difficulty is in formatting the output correctly for each of the different options so that it streams right and fits on the screen. Here's the first few lines of the hexdump -C output for a Python .pyc file:

```
00000000  03 f3 0d 0a f0 b5 69 57  63 00 00 00 00 00 00 00  |......iWc.......|
00000010  00 03 00 00 00 40 00 00  00 73 3a 00 00 00 64 00  |.....@...s:...d.|
00000020  00 64 01 00 6c 00 00 6d  01 00 5a 01 00 01 64 00  |.d..l..m..Z...d.|
00000030  00 64 02 00 6c 02 00 6d  03 00 5a 03 00 01 64 03  |.d..l..m..Z...d.|
00000040  00 65 01 00 66 01 00 64  04 00 84 00 00 83 00 00  |.e..f..d........|
```

The man page for this "canonical" formatting states that it is

1.   Display input offset in hexadecimal. So 10 is not really 10 in decimal, it's in hex. Do you know hex?

2.   Sixteen space-separated, two-column, hexadecimal bytes. That's each byte converted to hex. How many columns represent one byte?

3.   The same sixteen bytes in %_p format, which looks like a Python format specifier but is particular to hexdump. You'll need to read the man page more to find out what it means.

Then hexdump can also receive input from the stdin input, which means you can pipe things into it like

```
echo "Hello There" | hexdump —C
```

which produces the following on my macOS system:

```
00000000  48 65 6c 6c 6f 20 54 68  65 72 65 0a               |Hello There.|
0000000c
```

Notice that last line with the c character? Need to find out what that is, I guess.

It's this formatting and output that's going to be difficult, and your game is to replicate it as best you can, which is why the beginning of this exercise dictated that you work in a test first manner. It will be much easier to create tests that feed data to your hexdump and compare it with the real hexdump until it starts working.

Study Drill

Research the od command, and see if your hexdump code can be reused for an implementation of od. If it can, then make a library that both of them use.

Further Study

There are people who advocate only doing test first development, but I believe that no technique works all the time. I prefer to write tests first when I'm testing the *interaction* of the software from the user's perspective. I will write tests that describe the user interacting with the software and then go make the software make it happen. This is what you did here since you were testing how the user sees output from your command line hexdump calls.

For other types of coding tasks, dictating whether to write a test first or the code first is ridiculous and just kills your ability to solve a problem. Automated tests are simply tools, and you are an intelligent person who has the authority to try to use tools however you think they will work best in each situation. Anyone telling you different is probably an abusive person who actually isn't that great at writing software.

tr

This exercise is continuing the study of doing TDD (test-driven development, a.k.a. test first–style development). It's important to know how to do this kind of programming since it is used in many places, but as mentioned before it does have its limitations. You'll be doing one more exercise using TDD while implementing the tr command. Be very sure that you are being strict about writing your test first, then the code, then audit both.

In the previous exercise I told you to build your test case and your code incrementally. This is usually the least error-prone method of development, but it doesn't help you get better at analyzing your own code. In this exercise you're going to do things slightly differently as I'll have you write a *whole* test case, audit it, then write the *whole* code, audit it, and confirm your audit by running the tests.

That means in this exercise your process is this:

1. TDD a test case, attempting to write most of it.

2. Audit the test case and confirm it is written correctly.

3. Run the tests to ensure they fail, but look for any syntax errors. You should not have syntax errors at this point.

4. Write the code for the test case, *but do not run the test*.

5. Audit your code, and try to see how many defects you find *before* you run your test.

You'll be using this procedure in the next exercise to track metrics on your auditing skills and your testing skills, and to be more controlled in how you write code.

Exercise Challenge

The tr tool is a useful way to translate character streams. Despite being very simple it can do some very complex things to characters. For example, you can use tr to get a frequency of words used in your history with one line:

```
history | tr —cs A–Za–z '\n' | tr A–Z a–z | sort | uniq —c | sort —rn
```

Seems amazing, but this one line was used by Doug McIlroy to contend that a similar program written by Donald Knuth was much too involved and long. Knuth's implementation was "10 pages" and constructed everything from scratch. Doug's single line just uses standard Unix tools to do the same thing. This demonstrates the power of both the Unix use of piped discrete tools and tr's capability to translate text.

Use the man page and anything else you can to figure out what the `tr` command does. There is also a Python project by the same name, but I'll tell you to avoid that until you've done your implementation so you can compare this project with it later. Also don't forget that you'll need a whole project for this, and it should have the tests done TDD style as I've described in the beginning.

A Criticism of 45-Minute Blocks

I want you to continue to use 45-minute blocks of time, but there is one significant criticism of this way of working: you can't get into extended concentration flow. Working in short blocks of time like this helps when you need to grind through a large amount of work and must pace yourself. This happens when the work is really boring and not fun. I'm having you use 45-minute blocks just to pace yourself, but we'll also be using them later to gather metrics about how you work in the blocks for analysis.

But I'll caution you that the very best programming is done in the zone, the flow, the groove. It's where you are sunk deep into concentration for hours at a time and lose all track of time until you look up at 5 a.m. and realize you were up all night. This kind of intense concentration is what makes programming very enjoyable for me, but it's really only sustainable when you are very interested in what you're doing. When you need to work on someone else's terrible code base, the zone tends to just not happen. In those cases you need a different strategy that paces your work and chips away at it without grinding you down. That's what the 45-minute blocks are for.

Finally, one way to build your ability to get in the zone and concentrate for hours is to start with a few short blocks of time, then slowly increase them until you can do it for longer periods of time. Keep doing 45-minute blocks, but if you simply forget yourself and end up hacking for hours on end, enjoy yourself. Nobody will say you did this wrong. That's actually normal.

Study Drills

1. How did this way of working feel? Do you prefer it or not? Try to articulate why, then read some of the current writings on TDD or it's cousin behavior-driven development (BDD).

2. Do you think you found more or fewer defects by working in a way that required auditing your own code first rather than building it incrementally? Make a guess and then write it down.

sh

Y ou are now going to continue your TDD-style process, but you'll add a small hack session to start. The best method for working in TDD is to actually not write the tests first but instead to work this way:

1. Spend 45 minutes doing a hack to study the problem. This is called a "spike" and is intended to iron out issues you may run into or research things you need to know.

2. Plan out what you'll probably need to implement with a TODO list.

3. Turn this plan into a TDD test.

4. Run the test to make sure it fails.

5. Write the code for the test, using what you learned from the spike.

6. Audit your code and test to confirm quality.

This process is what I see TDD fanatics actually use when pressed with a problem they haven't studied before. It is also much more practical to work out a fast hack to get your mind going and to study the problem and then get serious about the work. If anyone tells you this isn't TDD, just don't tell them you did a spike first. They'll never know.

Exercise Challenge

In this exercise you'll implement the shell part of the Unix sh tool. You use sh all day when you code, as it's what runs inside Terminal (PowerShell is different) and runs your other programs. Typically this will be bash, but it might be fish, csh, or zsh.

The sh tool is a *massive* program to implement as it also supports a full programming language to automate your system. We are not going to implement the programming language, just the command line process running part.

To complete this task you'll need the following libraries:

1. subprocess (https://docs.python.org/2/library/subprocess.html) to launch other programs

2. readline (https://docs.python.org/2/library/readline.html) to get input from the user and support history

You aren't making a full Unix sh with piping and everything, but you could implement nearly everything except the programming language. Your implementation should be able to do the following:

1. Start with a prompt using readline and take a command to run from the user.

2. Parse the command into executable and arguments.

3. Use `subprocess` to launch the command with the arguments and control all the output.

To get started you can do your spike to study either `readline` or `subprocess` or both, whichever you think is necessary or unfamiliar. Once you do your spike then you start writing the tests and implementing the sytem.

Study Drill

Can you implement pipes? That's when you type `history | grep python` and the | sends the output of `history` to the input of `grep`.

Further Study

You can study my project python-lust (https://github.com/zedshaw/python-lust) if you want to learn even more about Unix process and resource management. It's not very large and is full of many little tricks.

diff and patch

To finish Part IV you will simply apply the full TDD process you've been studying on a much more involved project that may be unfamiliar to you. Refer back to Exercise 28 to confirm you know the process, and make sure you follow it strictly. Create a checklist to follow if you must.

WARNING! When you are actually working, all this strict process is not very useful. Currently you are studying the process and working on internalizing it so you can use it in the real world. That's why I am being strict about how you should follow it. This is only practice, so don't become a zealot about it when you are doing real work. The purpose of the book is to teach you a set of strategies to get work done, not teach you a religious rite you can preach to the masses.

Exercise Challenge

The diff command takes two files and produces a third file (or output) that encodes what changed in the first to make the second. It's the basis of tools like git and other revision control tools. Implementing diff in Python is fairly trivial since there's a library that does it for you, so you don't need to work on the algorithms (which can be very complex).

The patch tool is the companion to the diff tool as it takes a .diff file and applies it to another file to produce the third file. This lets you take changes you've made in two files, run diff to produce only the changes, then send that .diff file to someone. That person can then use their original copy of the file and your .diff with patch to rebuild your changes.

Here's an example work flow to demonstrate how diff and patch work. I have two files, A.txt and B.txt. The A.txt file contains some simple text, and then I copied it and created B.txt with some modifications:

```
$ diff A.txt B.txt > AB.diff
$ cat AB.diff
2,4c2,4
< her fleece was white a mud
< and every where that marry
< her lamb would chew cud
---
> her fleece was white a snow
> and every where that marry went
> her lamb was sure to go
```

This produces the file AB.diff that has changes from A.txt to B.txt, which you can see is fixing a rhyme I broke. Once you have this AB.diff you can use patch to apply the changes:

```
$ patch A.txt AB.diff
$ diff A.txt B.txt
```

That final command should *show no output* since the patch command before it effectively made A.txt have the same contents as B.txt.

Implementing these two should start with the diff command since you have a fully implemented diff using Python to cheat from. You can find it at the end of the difflib documentation (https://docs.python.org/ 2/library/difflib.html#a-command-line-interface-to-difflib) but try to implement your version and see how it compares to theirs.

The real meat of this exercise is the patch tool, which Python does not implement for you. You will want to read up on the SequenceMatcher class in difflib and specifically look at the Sequence-Match.get_opcodes function (https://docs.python.org/2/library/difflib.html#difflib.SequenceMatcher. get_opcodes). That is your only clue to making patch work, but it's a very good clue.

Study Drill

How far can you take this diff and patch combination? Can you combine them into one tool? Can you make it work like a miniature git?

Further Study

Find as many diff algorithms as you can. Another thing to research is how a tool like git works.

PART V
Parsing Text

This part of the book will teach you about text processing and, specifically, the beginning of parsing text formally. I won't get into all of the different theoretical elements of programming language theory since that is an entire university degree. This is merely the beginning of simple and naïve parsing of text in a way that you can use in many programming situations.

Most programmers have a strange relationship with parsing text. The core of all computer programming is parsing, and it's one of the most well understood and formalized aspects of computer science. Parsing data is everywhere in computing. You'll find it in network protocols, compilers, spreadsheets, servers, text editors, graphics renderers, and nearly anything that has to interface with a human or another computer. Even when two computers are sending a fixed binary protocol there is *still* an aspect of parsing involved despite the lack of text.

I'm going to teach you parsing because it's an easily understood solid technique that produces reliable results. When you're faced with processing some input reliably and giving accurate errors you'll turn to a parser rather than trying to write one by hand. Additionally, once you learn the basics of parsing it becomes easier to learn new programming languages because you can understand their grammar.

Introducing Code Coverage

In this part you should still be attempting to break and take apart any code you write. The new thing I'm adding in this part is the concept of code coverage. The idea of code coverage is you actually have no idea if you've tested most scenarios when you write your automated tests. You could use formal logic to develop a theory that you've covered everything, but as we know the human brain is incredibly terrible at finding flaws in its own thinking. This is why you use a cycle of "create then critique" during this book. It's simply too difficult for you to analyze your own thinking while you're also trying to create something.

Code coverage is a way to at *least* get an idea of what you've tested in your application. It won't find all your flaws, but it will at least show that you've hit every code branch you possibly can. Without coverage you actually have no idea if you've tested each branch. A very good example is handling failures. Most automated tests only test the most reliable conditions and never test error handling. When you run coverage you find out all the ways you forgot to test error handling code.

Code coverage also helps you avoid overtesting your code. I've worked on projects with test-driven development (TDD) enthusiasts who were proud of their 12/1 test/code ratios (meaning 12 lines of tests for every 1 line of code). A simple code coverage analysis showed that they were testing only 30% of the code, and many of those lines were tested the exact same way 6–20 times. Meanwhile, simple errors like exceptional conditions in database queries were completely untested and caused frequent errors. Eventually these kinds of test suites become an albatross that prevents project growth and simply eats up human work schedules. It's no wonder so many Agile consultancies hate code coverage.

During the videos in this exercise you'll see me running tests and using code coverage to confirm what I'm testing. You'll be required to do the same thing, and there are tools that will make this easy. I'll show you how to read the test coverage results and how to make sure you're efficiently testing everything you can. The goal is to have a thorough automated test suite but without wasted effort so you aren't testing just 30% of your code 12 times in a row.

Finite State Machines

Whenever you read a book on parsing there's this scary chapter on finite state machines (FSMs). They go into great detail of "edges" and "nodes" with every combination of possible "automata" being converted into other automata and frankly it's a bit much. There's a simpler explanation of FSMs that makes them practical and understandable while not violating the purist theoretical version of the same topic. Sure, you won't get a paper submitted to the ACM, because you don't know all of the mathematics behind FSM, but if you just want to use them in your applications then they are simple enough.

An FSM is a way to organize events happening to a set of states. Another way to define an event is an "input trigger," similar to the boolean expressions in an `if-statement`, but usually less complex. An event could be a button click, receiving a character from a stream, a change in the date or time, or pretty much anything you want to declare an event. A state is then any "position" your FSM stops at while it waits for more events, and at each state you redefine the allowed events (inputs). Events tend to be temporary, while states are usually fixed, and both are data that you can store. Finally, you can attach code to both events or states and even decide if code should run when you *enter* a state, during the state, or when exiting the state.

An FSM is simply a way to white-list the possible code to run when different events happen in different points in an execution. In an FSM, when you receive an unanticipated event, you get a failure because you have to explicitly say exactly what events (or conditions) are allowed at each state. An `if-statement` also handles possible branches, but it is a blacklist of possibilities. If you forget the `else` clause, then anything *not* covered by your `if-elif` conditions falls right through.

Let's break this down then:

1. You have states, which are a stored indicator of where the FSM is currently positioned. A state can be anything like "started," "key pressed," "aborted," or some similar way to describe how the FSM is positioned in its possible points of execution. Each state implies that it is waiting for something to happen before deciding what to do next.

2. You have events that can move the FSM from one state to another. An event can be "press a key," "socket connection fails," "file saved," or represent that some other external stimuli was received by the FSM so it must decide what to do and what state to enter next. An event can even just go back to the same state, which is how you loop.

3. FSMs transition from one state to another based on events happening, and only for the exact events given for that state (though one of the events can be defined as "any event"). They don't "accidentally" shift state, and you can track exactly how they moved from one state to another by looking at the events received and the states visited. This makes them very easy to debug.

4.   You have code that can run on each event before, after, and during a state transition. This means that you can run some code when an event is received, then decide what do to based on that event in the state, then run code again before you leave that state. This capability to execute code makes FSM very powerful.

5.   Sometimes "nothing" is also an event. This is powerful because it means you can transition an FSM to a new state even though nothing happened. However, in practical terms "nothing" tends to be the implied event "go again" or "wake up." In other situations nothing means "not sure yet, maybe the next event will tell me what state."

The power of the FSM comes in being able to explicitly state each event and that the events are simply data being received. This makes them incredibly easy to debug, test, and make correct since you know exactly each state possible and what can happen in each state for each event. In this exercise you're going to study an implementation of an FSM library and an FSM that uses it to understand how they work.

Exercise Challenge

I've created an FSM module that handles a few simple events for processing connections to a web server. This is an imaginary FSM to give you an example for how you can write one quickly in Python. It is only the basic skeleton of processing connections that read and write from a socket, and it's missing a few important things, but this is just a small example for you to use.

fsm.py

```python
 1    def START():
 2        return LISTENING
 3
 4    def LISTENING(event):
 5        if event == "connect":
 6            return CONNECTED
 7        elif event == "error":
 8            return LISTENING
 9        else:
10            return ERROR
11
12    def CONNECTED(event):
13        if event == "accept":
14            return ACCEPTED
15        elif event == "close":
16            return CLOSED
17        else:
18            return ERROR
19
20    def ACCEPTED(event):
21        if event == "close":
22            return CLOSED
23        elif event == "read":
```

```
24              return READING(event)
25          elif event == "write":
26              return WRITING(event)
27          else:
28              return ERROR
29
30      def READING(event):
31          if event == "read":
32              return READING
33          elif event == "write":
34              return WRITING(event)
35          elif event == "close":
36              return CLOSED
37          else:
38              return ERROR
39
40      def WRITING(event):
41          if event == "read":
42              return READING(event)
43          elif event == "write":
44              return WRITING
45          elif event == "close":
46              return CLOSED
47          else:
48              return ERROR
49
50      def CLOSED(event):
51          return LISTENING(event)
52
53      def ERROR(event):
54          return ERROR
```

There is also a tiny test that shows you how to run this FSM:

test_fsm.py

```
1       import fsm
2
3       def test_basic_connection():
4           state = fsm.START()
5           script = ["connect", "accept", "read",
6                     "write", "close", "connect"]
7
8           for event in script:
9               print(event, ">>>", state)
10              state = state(event)
```

Your challenge in this exercise is to turn this sample module into a more robust and generic FSM Python class. You should use this as a set of clues as to how you can handle events coming in, how states can be Python functions, and how you can do implied transitions. See how sometimes I return the function for the next state, but other times I return a call to that state function? Try to figure out why I'm doing that as it's very important in an FSM.

To complete this challenge you'll need to study the Python `inspect` module (https://docs.python.org/3/library/inspect.html) to see what you can do with a Python object and class. There are special variables like `__dict__` as well as functions in `inspect` that help you look into a class or object and find a function.

You may also decide that you want to invert this design. You could have the events be functions in a subclass, and inside the events functions you check for the current `self.state` to determine what to do next. It all depends on what you are processing, whether you have more events or states, and what makes sense at the time.

Finally, you *could* go with a design where there is an FSMRunner class that simply knows how to run modules that are designed like this. This has some advantages over a single class that knows how to run instances of itself, but it also can have some problems. For example, how does the FSMRunner keep track of the current state? Is it put in the module or in the instance of FSMRunner?

Study Drills

1. Make your test more extensive and do an FSM for a totally different domain you're familiar with.

2. Add an ability to turn on logging of the event run in your implementation. One of the *biggest* advantages of using an FSM to process events is you can store and log all of the events and states an FSM has received. This lets you debug *why* it reached a state you don't like.

Further Study

You should definitely read up on the real math behind an FSM. My little example here is not a fully formalized version of the concept so that you can understand it.

Regular Expressions

A regular expression (regex) is a succinct way to encode how a sequence of characters should be matched in a string. They are normally thought of as "scary" but, as you know, anything wrapped in fear is usually just taught wrong. The reality of regular expressions is they are a set of about eight symbols that tell a computer how to match a pattern. Used simply they are easy to understand. Where people run into trouble is trying to use incredibly complex regular expressions where an actual parser would be better. Once you understand these eight symbols and the limitations of regular expressions you'll see they aren't scary at all.

I'm going to have you do some more memorization to prime your brain for the discussion. The important symbols to memorize are

^ *Anchor beginning* of the string. This will match only if the match starts right at the beginning.

$ *Anchor end* of the string. This will match only if it goes to the end.

. *Any one* char. Accept any single character input.

? *Optional previous.* The previous part of the regex is optional, so A? means an optional "A" character.

* *0 or more* previous any number of times. Take the previous part of the regex and accept it repeatedly or skip over it. A* will accept "AAAAAAA" or "BQEFT" since there are zero A characters in it.

+ *1 or more* previous at least once. Same as * but it only accepts if the regex has 1 or more of those characters. A+ will accept "AAAAAAA" but not "BQEFT".

[X-Y] *Class* (range) of characters from X–Y. Accepts any of the characters listed in the range from X to Y. Using [A-Z] is all capital English letters. There are \ short cuts for many common character ranges you can use instead of this.

() *Capture* this part of the regular expression for later. Many regular expression libraries are used to also replace, extract, or alter text. A capture will take the part of the regex inside the ( ), and save it for later use. Many libraries then let you reference these captures. If you did ([A-Z]+) that would capture one or more capital English letters.

The Python re library (https://docs.python.org/3/library/re.html) lists many more symbols, but most of them are some modifier to these eight or extra features not commonly found in regular expression libraries. You'll start by creating flash cards for these eight, focusing on the italic phrases (*anchor end*, *optional previous*) so you can recall them quickly and explain what they do.

Once you've memorized these symbols take the following regular expressions and translate them to English and use the Python re library to try the listed strings or any other strings you can think of.

"**.*BC?$**"   helloBC, helloB, helloA, helloBCX

"**[A-Za-z][0-9]+**"   A1232344, abc1234, 12345, b493034

"**^[0-9]?a*b?.$**"   0aaaax, aaab9, 9x, 88aabb, 9zzzz

"***_***"   "_____***", "_", "*****", "_"

"**A+B+C+[xyz]***"   AAAABBCCCCCCxyxyz, ABBBBCCCxxxx, ABABABxxxx

Once you've translated them, use the Python re module to try them out in the shell like this:

Exercise 31 Python Session

```
1    >>> import re
2    >>> m = re.match(r".*BC?$", "helloB").span()
3    >>> re.match(r".*BC?$", "helloB").span()
4    (0, 6)
5    >>> re.match(r"[A-Za-z][0-9]+", "A1232344").span()
6    (0, 8)
7    >>> re.match(r"[A-Za-z][0-9]+", "abc1234").span()
8    Traceback (most recent call last):
9      File "<stdin>", line 1, in <module>
10   AttributeError: 'NoneType' object has no attribute 'span'
11   >>> re.match(r"[A-Za-z][0-9]+", "1234").span()
12   Traceback (most recent call last):
13     File "<stdin>", line 1, in <module>
14   AttributeError: 'NoneType' object has no attribute 'span'
15   >>> re.match(r"[A-Za-z][0-9]+", "b493034").span()
16   (0, 7)
17   >>>
```

You'll get the AttributeError: 'NoneType' on any that do *not* match because the re.match function returns a None when it doesn't match your regex.

Exercise Challenge

The challenge is to attempt to use your FSM module to implement *one* simple regular expression that does at least three of these operations. This will be a difficult challenge, but use the Python re library to help you plan and test your implementation of this regular expression. Then, once you know how to do this, never do it again. Life is too short to do things computers are already good at doing.

Study Drills

1. Expand your flash cards to include every possible symbol in the Python re library documentation.

2. If you ever want to match a * char, then you can escape it with *. Most of the other symbols have this too.

3. Make sure you know how to use re.ASCII because some parsing requirements need it.

Further Study

Look at the regex library (https://pypi.python.org/pypi/regex/), which is better if you need Unicode support.

Scanners

My first book, *Learn Python 3 the Hard Way*, very casually covered scanners in Exercise 48, but now we're going to get more formal. I'll explain the concept behind scanning text, how that relates to regular expressions, and how you can create a little scanner for a tiny piece of Python code.

Let's use the following Python code as an example to start the discussion:

```python
def hello(x, y):
    print(x + y)

hello(10, 20)
```

You've been training in Python for a while, so your brain most likely can read this code quickly, but do you *really* understand what it is? When I (or someone else) taught you Python I had you memorize all the "symbols." The def and () characters are each symbols, but there needs to be a way for Python to process these that is reliable and consistent. Python also needs to be able to read hello and understand it's a "name" for something, and then later know the difference between def hello(x, y) and hello(10, 20). How does it do this?

The first step to doing this is scanning the text looking for "tokens." At the scanning phase a language like Python doesn't first care what's a symbol (def) and what's a name (hello). It will simply try to convert the input language into patterns of text called "tokens." It does this by applying a sequence of regular expressions that "match" each of the possible inputs that Python understands. You'll remember from Exercise 31 that a regular expression is a way to tell Python what sequences of characters to match or accept. All the Python interpreter does is use many regular expressions to match every token it understands.

If you look at the code above, you might be able to write a set of regular expressions to process it. You'd need a simple regex for def that's just "def." You'd need more for the ()+:, characters. You'd then be left with how to handle print, hello, 10, and 20.

Once you've identified all the symbols in the code sample above you need to name them. You can't just refer to them by their regex, since it's inefficient to look up and also confusing. Later you'll learn that giving each symbol its own name (or number) simplifies parsing, but for now, let's devise some names for these regex patterns. I could say def is simply DEF, then ()+:, can be LPAREN RPAREN PLUS COLON COMMA. After that I can call the regex for words like hello and print simply NAME. By doing this I'm coming up with a way to convert the stream of raw text someone enters into a stream of single number (or named) tokens to use in later stages.

Python is also tricky because it needs a leading whitespace regular expression to handle the indenting and dedenting of the code blocks. For now, let's just use a fairly dumb one of ^\s+ and then pretend that this also captures how many spaces were used at the beginning of the line.

Eventually you'd have a set of regular expressions that can handle the preceding code and it might look something like this:

Regex	Token
`def`	DEF
`[a-zA-Z_][a-zA-Z0-9_]*`	NAME
`[0-9]+`	INTEGER
`\(`	LPAREN
`\)`	RPAREN
`\+`	PLUS
`:`	COLON
`,`	COMMA
`^\s+`	INDENT

The job of a scanner is to take these regular expressions and use them to break the input text into a stream of identified symbols. If I do that to the code example I could produce this:

```
DEF NAME(hello) LPAREN NAME(x) COMMA NAME(y) RPAREN COLON
INDENT(4) NAME(print) LPAREN NAME(x) PLUS NAME(y) RPAREN
NAME(hello) RPAREN INTEGER(10) COMMA INTEGER(20) RPAREN
```

Study this transformation, matching each line of this scanner output, and compare it to the previous Python code using the regular expressions in the table. You'll see that this is simply taking the input text and matching each regex to the token name and then saving any information needed like `hello` or the number `10`.

Puny Python Scanner

I've written a very small Puny Python script that demonstrates scanning this tiny Puny Python language:

ex32.py

```
1    import re
2
3    code = [
4    "def hello(x, y):",
5    "    print(x + y)",
6    "hello(10, 20)",
7    ]
8
9    TOKENS = [
10   (re.compile(r"^def"),                    "DEF"),
```

```
11      (re.compile(r"^[a-zA-Z_][a-zA-Z0-9_]*"),   "NAME"),
12      (re.compile(r"^[0-9]+"),                   "INTEGER"),
13      (re.compile(r"^\("),                       "LPAREN"),
14      (re.compile(r"^\)"),                       "RPAREN"),
15      (re.compile(r"^\+"),                       "PLUS"),
16      (re.compile(r"^:"),                        "COLON"),
17      (re.compile(r"^,"),                        "COMMA"),
18      (re.compile(r"^\s+"),                      "INDENT"),
19      ]
20
21      def match(i, line):
22          start = line[i:]
23          for regex, token in TOKENS:
24              match = regex.match(start)
25              if match:
26                  begin, end = match.span()
27                  return token, start[:end], end
28          return None, start, None
29
30      script = []
31
32      for line in code:
33          i = 0
34          while i < len(line):
35              token, string, end = match(i, line)
36              assert token, "Failed to match line %s" % string
37              if token:
38                  i += end
39                  script.append((token, string, i, end))
40
41      print(script)
```

When you run this script you get a list of tuples that are TOKEN, the matched string, beginning, and end, like this:

```
[('DEF', 'def', 3, 3), ('INDENT', ' ', 4, 1), ('NAME', 'hello', 9, 5),
('LPAREN', '(', 10, 1), ('NAME', 'x', 11, 1), ('COMMA', ',', 12, 1),
('INDENT', ' ', 13, 1), ('NAME', 'y', 14, 1), ('RPAREN', ')', 15, 1),
('COLON', ':', 16, 1), ('INDENT', '    ', 4, 4), ('NAME', 'print', 9, 5),
('LPAREN', '(', 10, 1), ('NAME', 'x', 11, 1), ('INDENT', ' ', 12, 1),
('PLUS', '+', 13, 1), ('INDENT', ' ', 14, 1), ('NAME', 'y', 15, 1),
('RPAREN', ')', 16, 1), ('NAME', 'hello', 5, 5), ('LPAREN', '(', 6, 1),
('INTEGER', '10', 8, 2), ('COMMA', ',', 9, 1), ('INDENT', ' ', 10, 1),
('INTEGER', '20', 12, 2), ('RPAREN', ')', 13, 1)]
```

This code is *definitely* not the fastest or most accurate scanner you can create. This is a simple script to demonstrate the basics of how a scanner works. For doing real scanning work you would use a tool to *generate* a scanner that's much more efficient. I cover that in the *Further Study* section.

Exercise Challenge

Your job is to take this sample scanner code and turn it into a generic Scanner class to use later. The goal of this Scanner class is to take an input file, scan it into this list of tokens, and then allow you to pull the tokens out in order. The API should have the following capabilities:

__init__ Takes a similar list of tuples (without the re.compile) and configures the scanner.

scan Takes a string and runs the scan on it, creating a list of tokens for later. You should keep this string around for people to access later.

match Given a list of possible tokens, returns the first one that matches the first token in the list and removes it.

peek Given a list of possible tokens, returns which ones *could* work with match but does not remove it from the list.

push Pushes a token back on the token stream so that a later peek or match will return it.

You should also create a generic Token class that replaces the tuple I'm using. It should be able to track the token found, the matched string, the beginning, and the end of where it matched in the original string.

Study Drills

1. Install the library pytest-cov and use it to measure the coverage of your automated tests.
2. Use the results of pytest-cov to improve your automated tests.

Further Study

The better way to create a scanner is to exploit the following three facts about regular expressions:

1. Regular expressions are finite state machines.
2. You can combine small finite state machines into larger more complex finite state machines accurately.
3. A combined finite state machine that matches many small regexes will operate the same as each of the regular expressions on their own and be more efficient.

There are many tools that use this fact to accept a scanner definition, turn each little regex into FSMs, and then combine them to produce one fast piece of code that can reliably match all the tokens. The advantage of this is you can feed these generated scanners individual characters in a rolling fashion and have them identify the tokens rapidly. This is preferred to the way I'm doing it here where I chunk up the string and try a sequence of regex in order until I find one.

Research how scanner generators work and compare them to what you've written.

Parsers

Imagine you're given a huge list of numbers and you have to enter them into a spreadsheet. At first, this huge list is just a raw stream of digits separated by spaces. Your brain automatically breaks the stream of digits at the spaces and creates numbers. That's your brain acting like a scanner. You then take the numbers and enter them into rows and columns that have meaning. Your brain is acting like a parser by taking the flat stream of numbers (tokens), and turning them into a 2-dimensional grid of more meaningful rows and columns. The rules you follow for what numbers go into what rows and what columns is your "grammar," and a parser's job is to enforce the grammar just like you would with a spreadsheet.

Let's look at the example Puny Python code from Exercise 32 one more time and discuss parsers from three different viewing angles:

```
def hello(x, y):
    print(x + y)

hello(10, 20)
```

When you look at this code what do you see? I see a tree, similar to the BSTree or TSTree we created earlier. Do you see the tree? Let's start at the very beginning of this file and learn how to go from the characters to a tree.

First, when we load a .py file it is just a stream of "characters"—actually bytes, but Python uses Unicode so characters will have to do. These characters are in a line, with zero structure to them, and the job of our scanner is to add the first level of meaning. The scanner does this by using regular expressions to *extract* meaning from the stream of characters, creating a list of tokens. We have gone from a list of characters to a list of tokens, but look at the def hello(x,y): function. That is a function with a block of code inside it. This means some form of "containment" or "thing inside a thing" structure.

A really easy way to represent containment is with a tree. We *could* use a table like your spreadsheet, but it's not as easy to work with as a tree. Look at the hello(x, y) part next. We have a NAME (hello) token, but we want to grab the contents of the (...) part and know that it is inside the parentheses. Again, we can use a tree, and we "nest" the x, y part inside the (...) part as a child or branch of the tree. Eventually we would have a tree starting at the root of this Python code, and each block, print, function definition, and function call would be branches from root, which would have children, and so on.

Why would we do this? We need to know the *structure* of the Python code based on its grammar so that we can analyze it later. If we don't convert the linear list of tokens into a tree structure, then we have no idea where the boundaries of functions, blocks, branches, or expressions are. We'll have to determine the boundaries on the fly in a "straight line" way, which isn't very easy to do reliably. Plenty of early terrible languages are straight line languages, and we now know they don't have to be. We can use a parser to build the tree structure.

The job of a parser is to take the list of tokens from the scanner and translate them into a more meaningful tree of grammar. You can think of a parser as applying another regular expression to the token stream. The scanner's regex boxes up chunks of characters into tokens. The parser's "regex" puts those tokens inside boxes, that have boxes inside them, and so on until the tokens are no longer linear.

The parser *also* adds meaning to these boxes. A parser would simply drop the parentheses tokens and just create a special `parameters` list for a possible `Function` class. It would drop colons, useless spaces, commas, any tokens that don't actually add meaning, and translate them into nested structures that are easier to process. The end result might look like this fake tree for the previous sample code:

```
* root
  * Function
    — name = hello
    — parameters = x, y
    — code:
      * Call
        — name = print
        — parameters =
            * Expression
              — Add
                — a = x
                — b = y
  * Call
    — name = hello
    — parameters = 10, 20
```

Study how I went from the sample Python code to this fictional tree that represents the code before you move on. It's not difficult to understand, but it's key that you be able to look at the Python code and figure out the tree structure.

Recursive Descent Parsing

There are a few established ways to create a parser for this kind of grammar, but the simplest to start with is called a recursive descent parser (RDP). I actually taught you this topic in *Learn Python 3 the Hard Way*, Exercise 49. You created a simple RDP parser to handle your little game language, and you didn't even know it. In this exercise I'll give a more formal description of how to write an RDP parser, then let you attempt it for our little snippet of Python above.

An RDP uses mutually recursive function calls that implement the tree structure of a given grammar. The code for an RDP parser looks like the actual grammar you're processing, and they're simple to write as long as you follow some rules. The two disadvantages of an RDP parser are that they might not be very efficient and you usually write them by hand, so they'll have more errors than a generated parser. There are also some theoretical limitations regarding what an RDP parser can parse, but since you write them by hand you can usually work around a lot of those limitations.

To write an RDP parser you need to process your scanner tokens using three main operations:

peek Return if the next token *could* match, but don't take it off the stream.

match Match the next token, taking it off the stream.

skip Skip the next token as it's not needed, taking it off the stream.

You'll notice these are the three operations I told you to create for your Scanner in Exercise 33, and this is why. You need them for doing an RDP parser.

You use these three functions to write grammar parsing functions that grab tokens from the scanner. A short example from this exercise is parsing this simple function:

```
def function_definition(tokens):
    skip(tokens) # discard def
    name = match(tokens, 'NAME')
    match(tokens, 'LPAREN')
    params = parameters(tokens)
    match(tokens, 'RPAREN')
    match(tokens, 'COLON')
    return {'type': 'FUNCDEF', 'name': name, 'params': params}
```

You can see I'm simply taking the tokens and using match and skip to process them. You'll also notice I have a parameters function, which is the "recursive" part of recursive descent parser. The function_definition calls parameters when it needs to parse the parameters to a function.

BNF Grammars

It's a little tricky to attempt to write an RDP parser from scratch without *some* form of specification of the grammar. Do you remember when I asked you to convert one regex into an FSM? It was hard, right? It required a *lot* more code than just the few characters in the regex. When you write the RDP parser for this exercise you'll be doing a similar thing, so it'll help to have a language that's "regex for grammars."

The most common "regex for grammars" is called a Backus–Naur Form (BNF), named after the creators John Backus and Peter Naur. A BNF describes the tokens required and how those tokens repeat to form the grammar for a language. BNF also uses the same symbols as regular expressions, so *, +, and ? have similar meanings.

For this exercise I'm going to use the IETF Augmented BNF syntax at https://tools.ietf.org/html/rfc5234 to specify the grammar for the Puny Python snippet. ABNF operators are mostly the same as regex except, for some odd reason, they put repetition *before* the thing to repeat, not after. Other than that, read the specification and try to figure out what the following means:

```
root = *(funccal / funcdef)
funcdef = DEF name LPAREN params RPAREN COLON body
funccall = name LPAREN params RPAREN
params = expression *(COMMA expression)
expression = name / plus / integer
plus = expression PLUS expression
PLUS = "+"
LPAREN = "("
RPAREN = ")"
COLON = ":"
COMMA = ","
DEF = "def"
```

Let's look at only the `funcdef` line and compare it to the `function_definition` Python code we have above, matching each part:

funcdef = This we replicate with the `def function_definition(tokens)`, and it starts this part of our grammar.

DEF This is specified in the grammar as `DEF = "def"`, and in the Python code I just skip it with `skip(tokens)`.

name I need this, so I match it with `name = match(tokens, 'NAME')`. I use the convention of CAPITALS to indicate things in the BNF I most likely will skip.

LPAREN I assumed I received a `def`, but now I want to enforce a `(` so I match it, but I ignore the result using `match(tokens, 'LPAREN')`. It's like "required but skipped."

params In the BNF I define `params` as a new "grammar production" or "grammar rule." That means in my Python code I need a new function. In this function, I can call that function with `params = parameters(tokens)`. Later I define the `parameters` function to process comma-separated parameters for functions.

RPAREN I discard this but require it again with `match(tokens, 'RPAREN')`.

COLON Once again, I discard the match `match(tokens, 'COLON')`.

body I'm actually skipping the body here because Python's indented syntax is a little too hard for this simple example code. You will need to handle this problem in the exercise unless you feel like going for it.

That is basically how you read an ABNF specification and systematically translate it into code. You start at the root, implement each grammar production as a function, and leave the scanner to handle the simple tokens (which I denote with CAPITAL letters).

Quick Demo Hack Parser

Here's my quick hack RDP parser that you can use to base your more formal and clean parser on:

ex33.py

```python
1   from scanner import *
2   from pprint import pprint
3
4   def root(tokens):
5       """root = *(funccal / funcdef)"""
6       first = peek(tokens)
7
8       if first == 'DEF':
9           return function_definition(tokens)
10      elif first == 'NAME':
11          name = match(tokens, 'NAME')
12          second = peek(tokens)
13
14          if second == 'LPAREN':
15              return function_call(tokens, name)
16          else:
17              assert False, "Not a FUNCDEF or FUNCCALL"
18
19  def function_definition(tokens):
20      """
21      funcdef = DEF name LPAREN params RPAREN COLON body
22      I ignore body for this example 'cause that's hard.
23      I mean, so you can learn how to do it.
24      """
25      skip(tokens) # discard def
26      name = match(tokens, 'NAME')
27      match(tokens, 'LPAREN')
28      params = parameters(tokens)
29      match(tokens, 'RPAREN')
30      match(tokens, 'COLON')
31      return {'type': 'FUNCDEF', 'name': name, 'params': params}
32
33  def parameters(tokens):
34      """params = expression *(COMMA expression)"""
35      params = []
36      start = peek(tokens)
37      while start != 'RPAREN':
38          params.append(expression(tokens))
39          start = peek(tokens)
40          if start != 'RPAREN':
41              assert match(tokens, 'COMMA')
42      return params
43
44  def function_call(tokens, name):
```

```
45          """funccall = name LPAREN params RPAREN"""
46          match(tokens, 'LPAREN')
47          params = parameters(tokens)
48          match(tokens, 'RPAREN')
49          return {'type': 'FUNCCALL', 'name': name, 'params': params}
50
51      def expression(tokens):
52          """expression = name / plus / integer"""
53          start = peek(tokens)
54
55          if start == 'NAME':
56              name = match(tokens, 'NAME')
57              if peek(tokens) == 'PLUS':
58                  return plus(tokens, name)
59              else:
60                  return name
61          elif start == 'INTEGER':
62              number = match(tokens, 'INTEGER')
63              if peek(tokens) == 'PLUS':
64                  return plus(tokens, number)
65              else:
66                  return number
67          else:
68              assert False, "Syntax error %r" % start
69
70      def plus(tokens, left):
71          """plus = expression PLUS expression"""
72          match(tokens, 'PLUS')
73          right = expression(tokens)
74          return {'type': 'PLUS', 'left': left, 'right': right}
75
76
77      def main(tokens):
78          results = []
79          while tokens:
80              results.append(root(tokens))
81          return results
82
83      parsed = main(scan(code))
84      pprint(parsed)
```

You'll notice I'm using a scanner module I wrote that has my match, peek, skip, and scan functions. I use a from scanner import * only to make this example more understandable. You should use your Scanner class.

You'll notice that I put my ABNF for this little parser in the documentation comments to each function. This helped me write each parser code and could be used for error reporting later. You should study this parser, possibly even as a master copy, before you attempt the *Exercise Challenge*.

Exercise Challenge

Your next challenge is to combine *your* Scanner class with a freshly written Parser class that you can subclass and re-implement with my simple parser here. Your base Parser class should be able to

1. Take a Scanner object and execute itself. You can assume any default function is the start of a grammar.

2. Have error handling code that is better than my simple assert usage here.

You should then implement PunyPythonPython, which can parse just this tiny little Python language and do the following:

1. Instead of just producing a list of dicts, you should create classes for each grammar production result. These classes then become objects inside a list.

2. The classes only need to store the tokens that are parsed, but be prepared to do more later.

3. You only have to parse this little language, but you should attempt to solve the "Python indent" problem. You *might* have to change the Scanner to be smart about only matching INDENT whitespace at the beginning of a line, and ignoring it everywhere else. You will also need to keep track of how *much* you've indented, and also record a 0 indent so you can "dedent" the blocks.

An extensive test suite would involve handing more samples of this tiny little python to the parser, but for now just get this one little file to parse. Try to have good coverage in the test and exploit as many errors as you can.

Study Drill

This exercise is *huge*, so just get it done. Take your time, and chip away at this a little at a time. I highly recommend studying my tiny sample here until you've fully figured it out and also printing out the tokens being processed at key points.

Further Study

Check out the SLY Parser Generator by David Beazley (http://sly.readthedocs.io/en/latest/) for a way to have a computer figure out your parser and scanner (a.k.a. lexer) for you. Feel free to attempt to replicate this exercise with SLY for comparison.

Analyzers

Yfrom the ou now have a parser that should be producing a tree of grammar production objects. I'll call this your "parse tree," and it means you can analyze the whole program by starting at the top of the parse tree and then "walking" it until you've visited every node. You've done something like this when you were learning about the BSTree and TSTree data structures. You started at the top and visited each node, and the order you visited them in (depth-first, breadth-first, in-order, etc.) determined how the nodes were processed. Your parse tree has the same capability, and your next step in writing the little Python interpreter is to walk the tree and analyze it.

The analyzer's job is to find semantic mistakes in your grammar and to fix or add information the next stage needs. The semantic mistakes are errors that, while grammatically correct, don't make sense as a Python program. This can be anything from a variable that hasn't been defined yet to non-sequitur code that simply makes no sense. Some language grammars are so loose the analyzer has to do more work to fix the parse tree. Other languages are so easy to parse and process that they don't even need an analyzer step.

To write an analyzer you'll need a way to visit each node in your parse tree, analyze it for errors, and fix any missing information. There are three general ways you can do this:

1. You create an analyzer that knows how to update each grammar production. It will walk the parse tree in a similar way as your Parser did, with a function for each type of production, but its job is to alter, update, and check the productions.

2. You change your grammar productions so *they* know how to analyze their own state. Then your analyzer is simply an engine that walks the parse tree calling each production's analyze() method. With this style you'll need some state that is passed around to each grammar production class, which should be a third class.

3. You create a separate set of classes that implement the final analyzed tree you can hand to an interpreter. In many ways you'd mirror the parser's grammar productions with a set of new classes that take a global state and a grammar production, and configure their __init__ so that they're the analyzed result.

I recommend either item 2 or item 3 for your *Exercise Challenge* today.

Visitor Pattern

The "visitor pattern" is a very common technique in object-oriented languages where you create classes that know what they should do when "visited." This lets you centralize the code for processing a class to that class. The advantage of this is you don't need large `if-statements` that check types on classes to know what to do. Instead, you just create a class similar to this:

```
class Foo(object):
    def visit(self, data):
        # do stuff to self for foo
```

Once you have this class (and `visit` can be called anything), you then just go through a list and call it:

```
for action in list_of_actions:
    action.visit(data)
```

You'll use this pattern for both item 2 and item 3 styles of analyzers; the only difference is the following:

1.   If you decide that your grammar productions will also be the analysis results, then your `analyze()` function (that's our `visit()`) simply stores that data in the production class *or* in a state that's given to it.

2.   If you decide that your grammar productions will produce *another* set of classes for the interpreter (see Exercise 35), then each call to `analyze` will return a new object that you put into a list for later, or attach as children to the current object.

I'm going to cover the first situation where your grammar productions are also your analyzer results. This works for our simple little Puny Python script, and you should follow along with this style. If you want to try the other design later then you can.

A Short Puny Python Analyzer

WARNING! You should stop here if you want to attempt to implement a visitor pattern for your grammar productions on your own. I'm going to give a fairly complete but simple example that is full of spoilers.

The concept behind a visitor pattern seems bizarre, but it makes total sense. Each grammar production knows what it should be doing at different stages, so you might as well keep the code for that stage near the data it needs. To demonstrate this I've written a small dummy `PunyPyAnalyzer` that simply prints out the parse using the visitor pattern. I'm only doing one *sample* grammar production so you can understand how this is done. I don't want to give you too many clues.

The first thing I do is define a `Production` class that all of my grammar productions will inherit from.

```
1    class Production(object):
2        def analyze(self, world):
3            """Implement your analyzer here."""
```

This has my initial `analyze()` method and takes the `PunyPyWorld` we'll use later. The first example grammar production is a `FuncCall` production:

```
1    class FuncCall(Production):
2
3        def __init__(self, name, params):
4            self.name = name
5            self.params = params
6
7        def analyze(self, world):
8            print("> FuncCall: ", self.name)
9            self.params.analyze(world)
```

Function calls have a name and a `params`, which is a `Parameters` production class for the function call's parameters. Look at the `analyze()` method and you'll see the first visitor function. When you get to the PunyPyAnalyzer you'll see how this is run, but notice this function then calls `param.analyze(world)` on each of this function's parameters:

```
1    class Parameters(Production):
2
3        def __init__(self, expressions):
4            self.expressions = expressions
5
6        def analyze(self, world):
7            print(">> Parameters: ")
8            for expr in self.expressions:
9                expr.analyze(world)
```

That leads to the `Parameters` class, which contains each of the expressions that make up the parameters to the function. The `Parameters.analyze` simply goes through its list of expressions, of which we have two:

```
1    class Expr(Production): pass
2
3    class IntExpr(Expr):
4        def __init__(self, integer):
5            self.integer = integer
6
7        def analyze(self, world):
8            print(">>>> IntExpr: ", self.integer)
9
```

```
10      class AddExpr(Expr):
11          def __init__(self, left, right):
12              self.left = left
13              self.right = right
14
15          def analyze(self, world):
16              print(">>> AddExpr: ")
17              self.left.analyze(world)
18              self.right.analyze(world)
```

In this example I'm only adding two numbers, but I create a base Expr class and then an IntExpr and AddExpr class to do it. Each of these simply have analyze() methods that print out their contents.

With that we have the classes for our parse trees, and we can do some analysis. The first thing we need is a world that can keep track of variable definitions, functions, and other things our Production .analyze() methods need.

ex34a.py

```
1      class PunyPyWorld(object):
2
3          def __init__(self, variables):
4              self.variables = variables
5              self.functions = {}
```

When any Production.analyze() method is called, a PunyPyWorld object is passed to it so the analyze() method knows the state of the world. It can update variables, look for functions, and do anything else needed in the world.

We then need a PunyPyAnalyzer that can take a parse tree and the world and make all the grammar productions run:

ex34a.py

```
1      class PunyPyAnalyzer(object):
2          def __init__(self, parse_tree, world):
3              self.parse_tree = parse_tree
4              self.world = world
5
6          def analyze(self):
7              for node in self.parse_tree:
8                  node.analyze(self.world)
```

This is easy enough to then set up for a simple call to the function hello(10 + 20):

ex34a.py

```
1      variables = {}
2      world = PunyPyWorld(variables)
3      # simulate hello(10 + 20)
4      script = [FuncCall("hello",
5                  Parameters(
6                      [AddExpr(IntExpr(10), IntExpr(20))])
```

```
7                      )]
8     analyzer = PunyPyAnalyzer(script, world)
9     analyzer.analyze()
```

Be sure you understand how I structured that script variable. Notice how there's a list as the first thing?

Parser versus Analyzer

In this example I'm assuming the PunyPyParser has converted the NUMBER tokents to integers. In other languages you might leave only the tokens and have the PunyPyAnalyzer do the work of conversion. It all depends on where you want the errors to be, and where you can do the most useful analysis. If you put the work in the parser, then you can give early errors on formatting right away. If you put it in the analyzer, then you can give errors that use the entire parsed file to help.

Exercise Challenge

The point of all these analyze() methods is not to just print things out but instead to change the internal state of each Production subclass so that the interpreter can run it like a script. Your job in this exercise is to take your grammar production classes (which might be different from mine) and make them analyze.

Feel free to steal my starting point. You can take my analyzer and my world if you need, but you should have attempted to write your own first. You should also compare your production classes from Exercise 33 to mine. Are yours better? Can they support this design? Change them if they can't.

Your analyzer will need to do a few things for the interpreter to work correctly:

1. Keep track of variable definitions. In a real language this would require some very complicated nested tables, but for Puny Python just assume there's one giant table (a TSTree or dict) that all variables are in. This means the x and y parameters to the hello(x, y) function are actually global variables.

2. Keep track of where functions are so you can run them later. Our Puny Python is going to just have simple functions that you can run, but when the interpreter runs it needs to "jump" to them and run them. The best way to do that is to keep them around for later.

3. Check for any errors you can think of, such as missing variables in usage. This is tricky because a language like Python does more error checking in the interpreter stage. You should decide what errors are possible during analysis and implement them. For example, if I tried to use a variable that has not been defined what happens?

4. If you've implemented Python INDENT syntax correctly, then your FuncCall productions should have their attached code. The interpreter is going to need that to run it, so make sure there's a way to get to it.

Study Drills

1. This exercise is fairly hard already, but how would you create a better way to store variables that implements at least one more level of scope? Remember "scope" is the idea that the x, y in hello(x, y) do not impact an x or y variable you define outside the hello function.

2. Implement assignment in your scanner, parser, and analyzer. That means I should be able to do x = 10 + 14 and you can handle it.

Further Study

Research the difference between "expression-based" and "statement-based" programming languages. The short version is some languages have only expressions, so everything has some kind of return value associated with it. Other languages have expressions that have value and statements that have no value, so assigning variables to them should fail. Which kind of language is Python?

Interpreters

This final exercise in parsing should be both challenging and fun. You finally get to see your Puny Python script run and do something. It is quite alright to be struggling with this section and the concept of parsing. If you find that you've reached this point and you don't quite understand what's going on, take a step back and consider doing the exercises in this part again. Repeating this section a couple times before you continue will help you in the last two exercises of Part V where you make your own little languages.

I am purposefully *not* including any code in this exercise so that you have to attempt it based on the description of how an interpreter works. You already have Python as a reference for how these little statements in our Puny Python example should operate. You know how to walk your parse tree with the visitor pattern. All that's left is for you to write an interpreter that can glue this all together and make your little script run.

Interpreters versus Compilers

In the world of programming languages you have languages that are interpreted, and ones that are compiled. A compiled language takes your input source and does the scanning, parsing, and analyzing phases like you've done here. A compiler then "emits" machine code based on this analysis by walking it and writing the bytes that a real computer (or fake one) needs to run the CPU. Some compilers add an additional step of translating the input source code to an "intermediate language" that is generic enough to then compile down to bytes for the machine. Compilers are normally identified because you typically can't just run them; first you have to run the source through the compiler, then execute the result. C is a classic compiler, and you run a C program like this:

```
$ cc ex1.c -o ex1
$ ./ex1
```

The cc command is the "c compiler," and you're saying to take the ex1.c file, scan, parse, and analyze it, then output the executable bytes to the ex1 file. Once you do that you then just run it like you would any other program.

An interpreter doesn't produce compiled bytecode that you run; instead it just runs the result of the analysis directly. It is "interpreting" the input language the same way a bilingual person might interpret my English to my friend's Thai. It loads the source file, then scans, parses, and analyzes it just like a compiler does. Then it simply uses the interpreter's own language (in this case, Python) to run it based on the analysis.

If we were to implement a JavaScript interpreter in Python we would be "interpreting JavaScript with Python." JavaScript is my English, and an interpreter is interpreting it into Python (Thai) for me on the fly. If I wanted to interpret `1 + 2` from JavaScript using Python, I might do it like this:

1. Scan `1 + 2` and produce tokens `INT(1) PLUS INT(2)`.

2. Parse that into an expression `AddExpr(IntExpr(1), IntExpr(2))`.

3. Analyze that to convert the text 1 and 2 into actual Python integers.

4. Interpret that with the Python code `result = 1 + 2`, which I can pass to the rest of the parse tree.

By comparison, a compiler would do everything I did with steps 1 through 3, but then at step 4 it would write bytecode (machine code) to another file, which I can then run on the CPU.

Python Is Both

Python is a bit more modern and takes advantage of faster computers by almost doing both compilation *and* interpretation. It will work like an interpreter so you don't have to go through a compilation phase. But, interpreters are notoriously slow, so Python has an internal virtual machine of sorts. When you run a script like `python ex1.py`, Python actually runs it and compiles that to an `ex1.cpython-36.pyc` file in the `__pycache__` directory. That file is bytecode that the `python` program knows how to load and run, and it works kind of like fake machine code.

Your interpreter will never, and should never, be that fancy. Yours should just scan, parse, analyze, and interpret the Puny Python script.

How to Write an Interpreter

When you write an interpreter you are going to need to work between all three stages to fix things you missed or got wrong. I suggest that you get adding numbers to work first, then work on more complicated expressions until your script runs. I would appraoch it like this:

1. Add your first `interpret` method to the `AddExpr` class and have it just print out a message.

2. Get your interpreter to visit this class reliably, passing in the `PunyPyWorld` it needs.

3. Once you've got that you can get the `AddExpr.interpret` to do the job of calculating the addition of its two expressions and returning the result.

4. After that you then have to figure out where the results of this `interpret` step should go. To keep things simple, let's assume Puny Python is an expression-based language, so *everything* returns a value. In that case, calls to one interpreter always have a return that parent calls can use.

5.   Finally, since Puny Python is expression-based, you can have your interpreter print out the final result of its `interpret` call.

If you do that, you'll have the basics of your interpreter, and you can start to implement all the other `interpret` methods you need to make this run.

Exercise Challenge

Writing the interpreter for Puny Python should involve nothing more than writing another visitor pattern that goes through the analyzed parse tree doing what the parse tree says to do. Your only goal is to get this one tiny (puny, even) script to run. That seems stupid since this is just three lines of code, but it is three lines that cover a wide range of topics in programming languages: variables, addition, expression, function definitions, and function calls. If you implemented `if-statements` you'd almost have a working programming language.

Your job is to write a `PunyPyInterpreter` class that takes the `PunyPyWorld` and the results of running `PunyPyAnalyzer` to execute the script. You're going to have to implement `print` as something that simply prints its variables, but the rest of the code should be something you run as you go through each production class.

Study Drills

1.   Once you have a `PunyPyInterpreter`, you should implement `if-statements` and boolean expressions and then expand your set of language tests to make sure this works. Try to push this little Python interpreter as far as you can go.

2.   What would it take to make Puny Python have statements too?

Further Study

You should be able to now study the grammars and specifications for as many languages as you like. Go ahead and find some languages and study them, but do it using the source code to the language. You should also do a more complete study of the IETF ABNF specification at https://tools.ietf.org/html/rfc5234 to prepare you for the next two exercises.

Simple Calculator

This challenge is to create a simple algebraic calculator using everything you've learned about parsing. You'll need to devise a language for doing basic math with variables, create an ABNF for the language, and write the scanner, parser, analyzer, and interpreter for it. This may actually be overkill for a simple calculator language since there won't be any nested structures like functions, but do it anyway to understand the full process.

Exercise Challenge

A simple algebraic language can mean many things to different people, so I want you to play with the Unix command bc. Here's an example of me running the bc command:

```
$ bc
bc 1.06
Copyright 1991–1994, 1997, 1998, 2000 Free Software Foundation, Inc.
This is free software with ABSOLUTELY NO WARRANTY.
For details type 'warranty'.
x = 10
y = 11
j = x * y
j
110
```

You'll want to be able to create variables, enter numbers (both integers and floating point), and have as many operators as you can devise. You can most likely play with bc, or even Python's shell, and work out the ABNF for it as you go. Remember that your ABNF is almost pseudo-code and doesn't have to be formally correct, just close enough for you to create your scanner and parser.

Once you have a "sketch" of the grammar in ABNF form, you can sit down to create the scanner and parser. I would write a set of simple scripts that exercise what you think the language should do and then have your test suite run them through your calculator at each stage. Doing that makes it easier to test the calculator.

After you have the parser you should write an analyzer to solidify and check the input for semantic meaning. In a simple language like this it may be more than you need, but this is an exercise in completing the entire process with a small toy language. Remember that a big job for the analyzer is to keep track of variable definitions at different points in the script so they can be accessed by the interpreter during execution.

After you have your analyzer creating an executable parse tree you can then write an interpreter that runs it. As mentioned in Exercise 35, there are two ways you can write an interpreter. One has you creating a "machine" that knows how to run the grammar productions as a sequence of inputs. This treats your grammar production classes (Expression, Assignment, etc.) as if they are machine code and simply does what they contain. The other style for an OOP language like Python is to have each production class know how to run itself. In this style the classes are "smart" and, given their environment, simply do what they need to make things happen. You then just "walk" the list of grammar productions calling run until you run out of them.

Which one you choose determines where you have to store the state for your little interpreter. If you make an Interpreter class that simply executes production data objects, then the Interpreter can keep track of all the state and be the computer, but the language is harder to extend since you have to improve the Interpreter for every production class. If you have the production classes know how to execute their own code, then it's easy to extend the language, but you have to find a way to pass the state of the computer around between each production.

When working on this, I suggest you start with *only* a tiny expression, such as addition. Get that to work first for the whole system, from scanner all the way to running simple addition. Then, if you don't like this design you can throw it out and do it again with a different design. Once you have your design working, you can then extend the language with more features.

Study Drills

1. The best study drill for this is to create functions to perform calculations and return results. If you can do that then your design will probably work for a larger language.

2. The next thing to try is implementing flow control with if-statements and boolean checks. It's quite alright if this is too daunting, but give it a try.

Further Study

Research as much of the bc or Python language as you can. Try to find other grammar files to read and study, especially any IETF protocol descriptions. IETF specifications are about as exciting a read as wet toilet paper, but they are good practice.

Little BASIC

You are now going to take a trip back in time to my childhood and implement a BASIC interpreter. No, I don't mean BASIC as in "a really simple bland interpreter." I mean the programming language BASIC. It was one of the very first programming languages, originally created at Dartmouth by John Kemeny and Thomas Kurtz. This version of basic is called Dartmouth BASIC, and the code looked something like this from the Dartmouth BASIC Wikipedia page (https://en.wikipedia.org/wiki/Dartmouth_BASIC):

```
5 LET S = 0
10 MAT INPUT V
20 LET N = NUM
30 IF N = 0 THEN 99
40 FOR I = 1 TO N
45 LET S = S + V(I)
50 NEXT I
60 PRINT S/N
70 GO TO 5
99 END
```

Those numbers to the left are actually *manually* entered line numbers. You told BASIC a number for each line, and then you could loop by simply telling it to "GO TO" that line. This later became GOTO in other versions of BASIC and became a kind of symbol of that era of computing.

Later versions of BASIC are documented on the main BASIC Wikipedia page (https://en.wikipedia.org/wiki/BASIC), which shows a long evolution of the language into more and more—ahem—modern forms. After a while it picked up structure like C and Algol, then it got object-oriented, and today you can find fairly advanced versions of BASIC. Check out Gambas BASIC at http://gambas.sourceforge.net/en/main.html if you want to see a modern free BASIC.

Exercise Challenge

Your challenge is to implement an original BASIC interpreter—the one with the manual line numbers and all CAPS mainframe text style. You'll want to look at the main BASIC Wikipedia page for possible tokens and sample code and also read the Dartmouth BASIC Wikipedia page for more clues. Your interpreter should be able to handle as much of the original BASIC as possible and produce valid output.

When you attempt this I suggest trying to do simple math, printing, and keeping track of line numbers. After that I'd work on getting GOTO to function correctly. If you have that, then you can finish the rest and slowly develop a suite of test programs to make sure your interpreter works well.

Good luck! This could take you a while, but it should be so much fun. I could see myself spending months on something like this just adding silly features like graphics so I can create all those stupid little programs I made when I was a kid. I wrote so *much* BASIC code it definitely warped my brain to count line numbers. That's probably why I like Vim so much.

Study Drills

This exercise is difficult enough, but if you want some additional challenges, do the following:

1. Create an alternative interpreter that uses a parser generator like SLY (https://github.com/dabeaz/sly). Once you have the ABNF this may end up being much easier, but it could be harder with a language like BASIC. You'll have to do it and find out.

2. Try to make a version of "structured BASIC" that has functions, loops, `if-statements`, and everything you'd find in an older non-OOP language like C or Pascal. This is a *huge* task, so I suggest if you attempt it to *not* write an RDP parser by hand. Use a tool like SLY to generate your parser and save your brain for more important things.

PART VI
SQL and Object Relational Mapping

I n this part of the book we're going to cover something that doesn't quite fit into the rest of the book's structure but is a very necessary topic for junior developers to understand. Knowing how to structure data into a SQL (pronounced "sequel") database will teach you how to think logically about your data storage requirements. There's a long established method for deconstructing data, storing it efficiently, and accessing it. In recent years the development of NoSQL databases has made this different, but the basic concepts behind relational database design are still useful. Everywhere that you need to store data there's a need to structure it well and understand it.

Most of these exercises will involve you using a SQL database, so I recommend you download the `sqlite3` binary from the SQLite3 download database (https://www.sqlite.org/download.html) to work with if you do not already have it. We are using Python so this is already installed with most Python installations, but sometimes it is not available. If you can't run

```
>>> import sqlite3
```

in your Python shell, then your Python is not installed with `sqlite3` by default. You'll need to find out why it's missing, and most likely there's another package you have to install before you can use it inside Python.

Understanding SQL Is Understanding Tables

Before you begin the exercises for this part you'll need to fully understand a single concept that causes many SQL beginners problems:

EVERY SINGLE THING IN A SQL DATABASE IS A TABLE.

Burn this into your mind. By a "table" I mean exactly like a spreadsheet where there are rows on the left and columns across the top. Typically you'll name the columns by some type of data that goes into that column. Then each row represents a single thing you need to put into the table. This could be an account, a list of people and their information, food recipes, or even cars. Each row is a car, and each column is some attribute about that car you need to track.

This causes most programmers problems because we think in terms of tree-like structures. An object and another object inside it that has a list that has a dict that has strings mapped to data. We nest things inside, and that style of data structure doesn't fit into a table. To most programmers it seems like these two structures (tables and trees) can't coexist, but a tree and a table are actually very similar. You can take nearly any tree structure and map it onto nearly any matrix, but you have to understand another aspect of SQL databases: the relation.

A relation is how a SQL database becomes more useful than a spreadsheet. A spreadsheet may let you create a full set of sheets and put different types of data inside them, but they make it difficult to *link* these sheets together. A SQL database's entire purpose is to make you link tables together using either columns *or* other tables. The genius of a SQL database is it uses one structure (the table) to then construct nearly any kind of data structure you can imagine by letting you link them together.

We'll learn about relations in a SQL database, but the quick answer is that if you can make a tree of data then you can put that tree into one or more tables. At this stage in the book we can abbreviate the process of converting a set of related Python classes into SQL tables like this:

1. Make tables for all the classes.
2. Set id rows in the children pointing at the parents.
3. Create linking tables "between" any two classes that are linked through a list.

It is much more complicated than that, but that's the gist of what you do when converting a set of classes to SQL. In fact, the majority of what a system like Django does is a more complicated version of the above three things.

What You'll Learn

The purpose of this section is *not* to teach you how to be a SQL system administrator. If you want to do that job then I suggest you learn everything you can about Unix and then go get certified by a company that offers certification in their technology. Keep in mind that this is not a very fun job and is similar to babysitting a large nursery of cats. Cats, not kittens.

What you will learn by the end of Part VI is how SQL works on a basic level. This is a quick crash course in SQL that ends with you creating your own object relational mapper (ORM) similar to Django's. This section is only a jumping off point to understanding how SQL works and is intended to give you enough information to know what's going on in a system like Django.

If you would like to go beyond this section in your work I recommend *Joe Celko's SQL for Smarties, Fifth Edition* (Morgan Kaufmann, 2014), and time. Joe's book is large, but it is very complete and he is a master of SQL. Going through that book will make you very capable.

Introduction to SQL

T he best way to learn how to model and design solid data is to start with the very basic building blocks. The SQL style of database has been the standard for data modeling and storage for many decades. Once you know basic SQL you can easily use just about any NoSQL or object relational mapping (ORM) system out there. SQL is a very formal way to store, manipulate and access data that gives you a formal way to think about it. It's also not very difficult since the language is not Turing complete like a full programming language.

SQL is everywhere, and I'm not saying that because I want you to use it. It's just a fact. I bet you have some in your pocket right now. All Android phones and iPhones have easy access to a SQL database called SQLite, and many applications on your phone use it directly. It runs banks, hospitals, universities, governments, small businesses, and large ones; just about every computer and every person on the planet eventually touches something running SQL. SQL is an incredibly successful and solid technology.

The problem with SQL is it seems *everyone* hates its guts. It is a weird, obtuse kind of "non-language" that most programmers can't stand. It was designed long before any of these modern problems like "web scale" or object-oriented programming even existed. Despite being based on a solid mathematically built theory of operation, it gets enough wrong to be annoying. Trees? Nested objects and parent child relationships? SQL just laughs in your face and gives you a massive flat table saying, "You figure it out, bro."

Why should you learn SQL if everyone hates it so much? Because behind this supposed hate is a lack of understanding of what SQL is and how to use it. The NoSQL movement is partially a reaction to antiquated database servers and also a response to a fear of SQL borne from ignorance of how it works. By learning SQL, you actually will learn important theoretical concepts that apply to nearly every data storage system past and present.

No matter what the SQL haters claim, you should learn SQL because it is everywhere, and it's actually not that hard to learn enough to be educated about it. Becoming an educated SQL user will help you make informed decisions about what databases to use and whether to not use SQL, and will give you a deeper understanding of many of the systems you work with as a programmer.

What Is SQL?

I pronounce SQL "sequel" but you can also say "ess-queue-ell" if you want. SQL also stands for Structured Query Language, but by now nobody even cares about that since that was just a marketing ploy anyway. What SQL does is give you a language for interacting with data in a database. Its advantage, though, is that it closely matches a theory established many years ago defining properties of well-structured data. It's not exactly the same (which some detractors lament), but it's close enough to be useful.

How SQL works is that it understands fields that are in tables and how to find the data in the tables based on the contents of the fields. All SQL operations are then one of four general things you do to tables:

Create   Put data into tables.

Read   Query data out of a table.

Update   Change data already in a table.

Delete   Remove data from the table.

This has been given the acronym CRUD and is considered a fundamental set of features *every* data storage system must have. In fact, if you can't do one of these four in some way then there better be a very good reason.

One way I like to explain how SQL works is by comparing it to spreadsheet software like Excel:

- A database is a whole spreadsheet file.
- A table is a tab/sheet in the spreadsheet, with each one being given a name.
- A column is a column in both.
- A row is a row in both.
- SQL then gives you a language for doing CRUD operations on these to *produce new tables or alter existing ones*.

The last item is significant, and not understanding this causes people problems. SQL only knows tables, and every operation produces tables. It either "produces" a table by modifying an existing one, or it returns a new temporary table as your data set.

As you read this book, you'll begin to understand the significance of this design. For example, one of the reasons object-oriented languages are mismatched with SQL databases is that OOP languages are organized around graphs, but SQL wants to only return tables. Since it's possible to map nearly any graph to a table and vice versa, this works, but it puts the burden on the OOP language to do the translation. If SQL returned a nested data structure, then this wouldn't be a problem.

The Setup

We will use SQLite3 as a training tool for this section. SQLite3 is a complete database system that has the advantage of requiring almost no setup. You just download a binary and work it like most other scripting languages. Using this, you'll be able to learn SQL without getting stuck in the administrivia of administering a database server.

Installing SQLite3 is easy. You can do one of the following:

- Go to the SQLite3 download page (http://www.sqlite.org/download.html) and grab the binary for your platform. Look for "Precompiled Binaries for X," with X being your operating system of choice.

- Use your operating system's package manager to install it. If you're on Linux then you know what that means. If you're on macOS then first go get a package manager, and then use it to install SQLite3.

When you've got it installed, make sure you can start up a command line and run it. Here's a quick test for you to try:

```
$ sqlite3 test.db
SQLite version 3.7.8 2011-09-19 14:49:19
Enter ".help" for instructions
Enter SQL statements terminated with a ";"
sqlite> create table test (id);
sqlite> .quit
```

Look to see that the `test.db` file is there. If that works, then you're all set. You should make sure that your version of SQLite3 is the same as the one I have here: 3.7.8. Sometimes things won't work right with older versions.

Learning SQL Vocabulary

To get started learning SQL you'll want to create flash cards (or use Anki) for these SQL terms. In the exercises after this one you'll learn and apply each of these SQL words to different problems. The best way to think about the SQL language is everything ends up being a `Create`, `Read`, `Update`, or `Delete` operation. Even if a word is `INSERT` you'll still think of that as a `Create` operation because it will create data. At first, just spend some time memorizing these words and keep drilling them as you do the exercises for this section.

CREATE   Creates a database table that can store columns of data

INSERT   Adds rows to a database table, filling in the columns of data

UPDATE   Changes one or more columns in a table

DELETE   Deletes a row from a table

SELECT   Queries a table, or set of tables, and returns a temporary table with the results

DROP   Destroys a table

FROM   Frequently part of a SQL query to specify what tables or columns to use

IN   Used to indicate a set of elements

WHERE   Used with queries to say where something should come from

SET   Used with update to indicate which columns to set to what

SQL Grammar

You'll next want to make another set of cards for the important grammar constructs of SQL. There aren't too many of them, but write these up (or use Anki) and start drilling them now so that you learn the language faster. The grammar you're learning is the one for the SQLite3 database we'll be using in this book. It's a fairly common SQL grammar, but each database has different weird flavors that you'd have to learn. Once you learn this one it's easy to figure out what another database uses.

You'll want to visit the SQLite 3 definition page (https://sqlite.org/lang.html) to create the cards you need. This page lists out everything that SQLite understands, but just focus on the main statements I list above. Add any other words you do not understand. Their diagrams are a little complicated, but they are simply graphical views of the SQL BNF, which you learned about in Part V. If you don't remember ABNF go back through Part V and relearn it.

Further Study

1.   Go to the SQLite3 grammar list and browse through all of the available commands. Most of them won't make sense, but if any interest you then make cards for those as well.

2.   Drill these cards for the entire time that you're doing the remaining exercises.

Creating with SQL

When we talk about the acronym CRUD, the "C" stands for "create," and it doesn't just mean creating tables. It also means inserting data into the tables and using tables and inserts to link tables. Since we need some tables and some data to do the rest of CRUD (read, update, and delete) we'll start with learning how to do the most basic creation operations in SQL.

Creating Tables

In the introduction in Exercise 38, I said that you can do CRUD operations to the data inside tables. How do you make the tables in the first place? By doing CRUD on the database *schema*, and the first SQL statement to learn is CREATE:

ex1.sql

```
1    CREATE TABLE person (
2        id INTEGER PRIMARY KEY,
3        first_name TEXT,
4        last_name TEXT,
5        age INTEGER
6    );
```

You could put this all on one line, but I want to talk about each line, so it's on multiple ones. Here's what each line does:

Line 1   The start of the "CREATE TABLE," which gives the name of the table as person. You then put the fields you want inside parenthesis after this setup.

Line 2   An id column, which will be used to exactly identify each row. The format of a column is NAME TYPE, and in this case I'm saying I want an INTEGER that is also a PRIMARY KEY. Doing this tells SQLite3 to treat this column as special.

Lines 3–4   A first_name and a last_name column, which are both of type TEXT.

Line 5   An age column that is just a plain INTEGER.

Line 6   Ending of the list of columns with a closing parenthesis and then a semicolon character.

Creating a Multi-table Database

Creating one table isn't too useful. I want you to now make three tables that you can store data into:

ex2.sql

```
1    CREATE TABLE person (
2        id INTEGER PRIMARY KEY,
3        first_name TEXT,
4        last_name TEXT,
5        age INTEGER
6    );
7
8    CREATE TABLE pet (
9        id INTEGER PRIMARY KEY,
10       name TEXT,
11       breed TEXT,
12       age INTEGER,
13       dead INTEGER
14   );
15
16   CREATE TABLE person_pet (
17       person_id INTEGER,
18       pet_id INTEGER
19   );
```

In this file you are making tables for two types of data and then "linking" them together with a third table. People call these "linking" tables "relations," but very pedantic people with no lives call all tables "relations" and enjoy confusing people who just want to get their jobs done. In my book, tables that have data are "tables," and tables that link tables together are called "relations."

There isn't anything new here, except when you look at person_pet you'll see that I've made two columns: person_id and pet_id. How you would link two tables together is simply *insert* a row into person_pet that had the values of the two rows' id columns you wanted to connect. For example, if person contained a row with id=20 and pet had a row with id=98, then to say that person owned that pet, you would insert person_id=20, pet_id=98 into the person_pet relation (table).

We'll get into actually inserting data like this in the next few exercises.

Inserting Data

You have a couple tables to work with, so now I'll have you put some data into them using the INSERT command:

ex3.sql

```
1    INSERT INTO person (id, first_name, last_name, age)
2        VALUES (0, "Zed", "Shaw", 37);
3
4    INSERT INTO pet (id, name, breed, age, dead)
```

```
5        VALUES (0, "Fluffy", "Unicorn", 1000, 0);
6
7    INSERT INTO pet VALUES (1, "Gigantor", "Robot", 1, 1);
```

In this file I'm using two different forms of the INSERT command. The first form is the more explicit style and most likely the one you should use. It specifies the columns that will be inserted, followed by VALUES, then the data to include. Both of these lists (column names and values) go inside parentheses and are separated by commas.

The second version on line 7 is an abbreviated version that doesn't specify the columns and instead relies on the implicit order in the table. This form is dangerous since you don't know what column your statement is actually accessing, and some databases don't have reliable ordering for the columns. It's best to only use this form when you're really lazy.

Insert Referential Data

In the last section you filled in some tables with people and pets. The only thing that's missing is who owns what pets and that data goes into the person_pet table like this:

ex4.sql

```
1    INSERT INTO person_pet (person_id, pet_id) VALUES (0, 0);
2    INSERT INTO person_pet VALUES (0, 1);
```

Again I'm using the explicit format first, then the implicit format. How this works is I'm using the id values from the person row I want (in this case, 0) and the id from the pet rows I want (again, 0 for the Unicorn and 1 for the Dead Robot). I then insert one row into the person_pet relation table for each "connection" between a person and a pet.

Exercise Challenge

1. Make another database with other INTEGER and TEXT fields for other things a person might have.

2. In these tables I made a third relation table to link them. How would you get rid of this relation table person_pet and put that information right into person? What's the implication of this change?

3. If you can put one row into person_pet, can you put more than one? How would you record a crazy cat person with 50 cats?

4. Create another table for the cars people might own, and create its corresponding relation table.

5. Search for "sqlite3 datatypes" in your favorite search engine and read the "Datatypes In SQLite Version 3" document (https://sqlite.org/datatype3.html). Take notes on what types you can use and other things that seem important. We'll cover more later.

6.   Insert yourself and your pets (or imaginary pets like I have).

7.   If you changed the database in the last exercise to not have the `person_pet` table, then make a new database with that schema and insert the same information into it.

8.   Go back to the list of data types and take notes on what format you need for the different types. For example, note how many ways can you write TEXT data.

9.   Add the relationships for you and your pets.

10. Using this table, could a pet be owned by more than one person? Is that logically possible? What about the family dog? Wouldn't everyone in the family technically own it?

11. Given the above, and given that you have an alternative design that puts the `pet_id` in the `person` table, which design is better for this situation?

Further Study

Read the documentation for the SQLite3 CREATE command at https://sqlite.org/lang_createtable.html and then review as many other CREATE statements as you can. You should also read INSERT documentation at https://sqlite.org/lang_insert.html, which should lead you to many other pages to read.

Reading with SQL

Out of the CRUD matrix you only know create. You can create tables and you can create rows in those tables. I'll now show you how to read, or in the case of SQL, SELECT:

ex5.sql

```
1    SELECT * FROM person;
2
3    SELECT name, age FROM pet;
4
5    SELECT name, age FROM pet WHERE dead = 0;
6
7    SELECT * FROM person WHERE first_name != "Zed";
```

Here's what each of these lines does:

Line 1 This says "select all columns from person and return all rows." The format for SELECT is SELECT what FROM tables(s) WHERE (tests), and the WHERE clause is optional. The * (asterisk) character is what says you want all columns.

Line 3 In this one I'm only asking for two columns, name and age, from the pet table. It will return all rows.

Line 5 Now I'm looking for the same columns from the pet table, but I'm asking for *only* the rows where dead = 0. This gives me all the pets that are alive.

Line 7 Finally, I'm selecting all columns from person just like in the first line, but now I'm saying only if they do *not* equal "Zed." That WHERE clause is what determines which rows to return or not.

Select across Many Tables

Hopefully you're getting your head around selecting data out of tables. Always remember this: *SQL ONLY KNOWS TABLES. SQL LOVES TABLES. SQL ONLY RETURNS TABLES. TABLES. TABLES. TABLES. TABLES!* I repeat this in this rather crazy manner so that you will start to realize that what you know in programming isn't going to help. In programming you deal in graphs, and in SQL you deal in tables. They're related concepts, but the mental model is different.

Here's an example of where it becomes different. Imagine you want to know what pets Zed owns. You need to write a SELECT that looks in person and then "somehow" finds my pets. To do that you have to query the person_pet table to get the id columns you need. Here's how I'd do it:

```
1    SELECT pet.id, pet.name, pet.age, pet.dead
2        FROM pet, person_pet, person
3        WHERE
4        pet.id = person_pet.pet_id AND
5        person_pet.person_id = person.id AND
6        person.first_name = "Zed";
```

Now, this looks huge, but I'll break it down so you can see it's simply crafting a new table based on data in the three tables and the WHERE clause:

Line 1   I only want some columns from pet, so I specify them in the select. In the last exercise you used * to say "every column" but that's going to be a bad idea here. Instead, you want to be explicit and say what column from each table you want, and you do that by using table.column as in pet.name.

Line 2   To connect pet to person I need to go through the person_pet relation table. In SQL that means I need to list all three tables after the FROM.

Line 3   Start the WHERE clause.

Line 4   First, I connect pet to person_pet by the related id columns pet.id and person_pet.id.

Line 5   *AND* I need to connect person to person_pet in the same way. Now the database can search for only the rows where the id columns all match up, and those are the ones that are connected.

Line 6   *AND* I finally ask for only the pets that I own by adding a person.first_name test for my first name.

Exercise Challenge

1.   Write a query that finds all pets older than 10 years.

2.   Write a query to find all people younger than you. Do one that's older.

3.   Write a query that uses more than one test in the WHERE clause using the AND to write it. For example, WHERE first_name = "Zed" AND age > 30.

4.   Do another query that searches for rows using three columns and uses both AND and OR operators.

5.   This may be a mind-blowing, weird way to look at data if you already know a language like Python or Ruby. Take the time to model the same relationships using classes and objects, then map it to this setup.

6.   Do a query that finds your pets you've added thus far.

7.   Change the queries to use your `person.id` instead of the `person.name` like I've been doing.

8.   Go through the output from your run, and make sure you know what table is produced for which SQL commands and how they produced that output.

Further Study

Continue to deep dive into SQLite3 by reading the documentation for the SELECT command at https://sqlite.org/lang_select.html and also read the documentation for the EXPLAIN QUERY PLAN feature at https://sqlite.org/eqp.html. If you ever wonder why SQLite3 did something, EXPLAIN is your answer.

Updating with SQL

Y̲ou now know the CR parts of CRUD, which leaves the update and delete operations. As with all the other SQL commands, the UPDATE command follows a format similar to DELETE, but it changes the columns in rows instead of deleting them.

ex9.sql

```
1    UPDATE person SET first_name = "Hilarious Guy"
2        WHERE first_name = "Zed";
3
4    UPDATE pet SET name = "Fancy Pants"
5        WHERE id=0;
6
7    SELECT * FROM person;
8    SELECT * FROM pet;
```

In the above code I'm changing my name to "Hilarious Guy," since that's more accurate. And to demonstrate my new moniker I renamed my Unicorn to "Fancy Pants." He loves it.

This shouldn't be that hard to figure out but, just in case, I'm going to break the first one down:

1. Start with UPDATE and the table you're going to update, in this case `person`.

2. Next use SET to say what columns should be set to what values. You can change as many columns as you want as long as you separate them with commas like `first_name = "Zed"`, `last_name = "Shaw"`.

3. Then specify a WHERE clause that gives a SELECT style set of tests to do on each row. When the UPDATE finds a match, it does the update and SETs the columns to how you specified.

Updating Complex Data

In the last example I had you do a subquery in the UPDATE, and now you'll use it to change all the pets I own to be named "Zed's Pet."

ex10.sql

```
1    SELECT * FROM pet;
2
3    UPDATE pet SET name = "Zed's Pet" WHERE id IN (
4        SELECT pet.id
5        FROM pet, person_pet, person
6        WHERE
7        person.id = person_pet.person_id AND
```

```
 8          pet.id = person_pet.pet_id AND
 9          person.first_name = "Zed"
10    );
11
12    SELECT * FROM pet;
```

This is how you update one table based on information from another table. There are other ways to do the same thing, but this way is the easiest to understand for you right now.

Replacing Data

I'm going to show you an alternative way to insert data that helps with atomic replacement of rows. You don't necessarily need this too often, but it does help if you're having to replace whole records and don't want to do a more complicated UPDATE without resorting to transactions.

In this situation, I want to replace my record with another guy but keep the unique id. The problem is, I'd have to either do a DELETE/INSERT in a transaction to make it atomic, or I'd need to do a full UPDATE.

Another simpler way to do it is to use the REPLACE command, or add it as a modifier to INSERT. Here's some SQL where I first fail to insert the new record, then I use these two forms of REPLACE to do it:

ex11.sql

```
 1    /* This should fail because 0 is already taken. */
 2    INSERT INTO person (id, first_name, last_name, age)
 3        VALUES (0, 'Frank', 'Smith', 100);
 4
 5    /* We can force it by doing an INSERT OR REPLACE. */
 6    INSERT OR REPLACE INTO person (id, first_name, last_name, age)
 7        VALUES (0, 'Frank', 'Smith', 100);
 8
 9    SELECT * FROM person;
10
11    /* And shorthand for that is just REPLACE. */
12    REPLACE INTO person (id, first_name, last_name, age)
13        VALUES (0, 'Zed', 'Shaw', 37);
14
15    /* Now you can see I'm back. */
16    SELECT * FROM person;
```

Exercise Challenge

1. Use UPDATE to change my name back to "Zed" by my person.id.

2. Write an UPDATE that renames any dead animals to "DECEASED." If you try to say they are "DEAD" it'll fail because SQL will think you mean, "Set it to the column named 'DEAD,'" which isn't what you want.

3. Try using a subquery with this just like with DELETE.

4. Go to the "SQL As Understood By SQLite" page (http://www.sqlite.org/lang.html) and start reading through the docs for CREATE TABLE, DROP TABLE, INSERT, DELETE, SELECT, and UPDATE.

5. Try out some of the interesting things you find in these docs, and take notes on things you don't understand so you can research them more later.

Further Study

As usual, continue diving deep into the SQLite3 language by reading the documentation on UPDATE at https://sqlite.org/lang_update.html and related pages.

Deleting with SQL

This is the simplest exercise, but I want you to think for a second before typing the code in. If you had "SELECT * FROM" for SELECT, and "INSERT INTO" for INSERT, then how would you write the DELETE format? You can probably glance down, but try to guess at what it would be, then look.

ex7.sql

```
1     /* make sure there's dead pets */
2     SELECT name, age FROM pet WHERE dead = 1;
3
4     /* aww poor robot */
5     DELETE FROM pet WHERE dead = 1;
6
7     /* make sure the robot is gone */
8     SELECT * FROM pet;
9
10    /* let's resurrect the robot */
11    INSERT INTO pet VALUES (1, "Gigantor", "Robot", 1, 0);
12
13    /* the robot LIVES! */
14    SELECT * FROM pet;
```

I'm simply implementing a very complex update of the robot by deleting him and then putting the record back but with dead=0. In later exercises I'll show you how to use UPDATE to do this, so don't consider this to be the real way you'd do an update.

Most of the lines in this script are already familiar to you, with the exception of line 5. Here you have the DELETE, and it has nearly the same format as other commands. You give DELETE FROM table WHERE tests, and a way to think about it is being like a SELECT that removes rows. Anything that works in a WHERE clause will work here.

Deleting Using Other Tables

Remember I said, "DELETE is like SELECT, but it removes rows from the table." The limitation is you can only delete from one table at a time. That means to delete all of the pets you need to do some additional queries and then delete based on those.

One way you do this is with a subquery that selects the ids you want deleted based on a query you've already written. There are other ways to do this, but this is one you can do right now based on what you know:

```
1    DELETE FROM pet WHERE id IN (
2        SELECT pet.id
3        FROM pet, person_pet, person
4        WHERE
5        person.id = person_pet.person_id AND
6        pet.id = person_pet.pet_id AND
7        person.first_name = "Zed"
8    );
9
10   SELECT * FROM pet;
11   SELECT * FROM person_pet;
12
13   DELETE FROM person_pet
14       WHERE pet_id NOT IN (
15           SELECT id FROM pet
16       );
17
18   SELECT * FROM person_pet;
```

The lines 1–8 are a DELETE command that starts off normally, but then the WHERE clause uses IN to match id columns in pet to the table that's returned in the subquery. The subquery (also called a subselect) is then a normal SELECT, and it should look really similar to the ones you've done before when trying to find pets owned by people.

On lines 13–16 I then use a subquery to clear out the person_pet table of any pets that don't exist anymore by using NOT IN rather than IN.

How SQL does this is with the following process:

1. Runs the subquery in the parentheses at the end and builds a table with all the columns just like a normal SELECT.

2. Treats this table as a kind of temporary table to match pet.id columns against.

3. Goes through the pet table and deletes any row that has an id IN this temporary table.

Exercise Challenge

1. Combine all of ex2.sql through ex7.sql into one file and redo the above script so you just run this one new file to recreate the database.

2. Add onto the script to delete other pets, and insert them again with new values. Remember that this is *not* how you normally update records and is only for the exercise.

3. Practice writing SELECT commands and then putting them in a DELETE WHERE IN to remove those records found. Try deleting any dead pets owned by you.

4. Do the inverse and delete people who have dead pets.

5. Do you really need to delete dead pets? Why not just remove their relationship in `person_pet` and mark them dead? Write a query that removes dead pets from `person_pet`.

Further Study

You'll want to read the DELETE documentation at https://sqlite.org/lang_delete.html for completeness.

SQL Administration

The word "administration" is overloaded in databases. It can mean "making sure a PostgreSQL server keeps running," or it can mean "altering and migrating tables for new software deployments." In this exercise I'm *only* covering how to do simple schema alterations and migrations. Managing a full database server is outside the scope of this book.

Destroying and Altering Tables

You've already encountered DROP TABLE as a way to get rid of a table you've created. I'm going to show you another way to use it and also how to add or remove columns from a table with ALTER TABLE.

ex12.sql

```
1    /* Only drop table if it exists. */
2    DROP TABLE IF EXISTS person;
3
4    /* Create again to work with it. */
5    CREATE TABLE person (
6        id INTEGER PRIMARY KEY,
7        first_name TEXT,
8        last_name TEXT,
9        age INTEGER
10   );
11
12   /* Rename the table to peoples. */
13   ALTER TABLE person RENAME TO peoples;
14
15   /* Add a hatred column to peoples. */
16   ALTER TABLE peoples ADD COLUMN hatred INTEGER;
17
18   /* Rename peoples back to person. */
19   ALTER TABLE peoples RENAME TO person;
20
21   .schema person
22
23   /* We don't need that. */
24   DROP TABLE person;
```

I'm doing some fake changes to the tables to demonstrate the commands, but this is everything you can do in SQLite3 with the ALTER TABLE and DROP TABLE statements. I'll walk through this so you understand what's going on:

Line 2   Use the IF EXISTS modifier, and the table will be dropped only if it's already there. This suppresses the error you get when running your .sql script on a fresh database that has no tables.

Line 5   Just recreating the table again to work with it.

Line 13   Using ALTER TABLE to rename it to peoples.

Line 16   Add a new column hatred that is an INTEGER to the newly renamed table peoples.

Line 19   Rename peoples back to person because that's a dumb name for a table.

Line 21   Dump the schema for person so you can see it has the new hatred column.

Line 24   Drop the table to clean up after this exercise.

Migrating and Evolving Data

Let's apply some of the skills you have learned. I'll have you take your database and "evolve" the schema to a different form. You'll need to make sure you know the previous exercise well and have your code.sql working. If you don't have either of these, then go back and get everything straightened out.

To make sure you are in the right state to attempt this exercise, when you run your code.sql you should be able to run .schema like this:

Exercise 13 Session

```
$ sqlite3 ex13.db < code.sql
$ sqlite3 ex13.db .schema
CREATE TABLE person (
    id INTEGER PRIMARY KEY,
    first_name TEXT,
    last_name TEXT,
    age INTEGER
);
CREATE TABLE person_pet (
    person_id INTEGER,
    pet_id INTEGER
);
CREATE TABLE pet (
    id INTEGER PRIMARY KEY,
    name TEXT,
    breed TEXT,
    age INTEGER,
    dead INTEGER,
    dob DATETIME
);
```

Make sure your tables look like my tables, and if not, then go back and remove any commands that are doing ALTER TABLE or anything from the last exercise.

Exercise Challenge

What you're tasked with doing is the following list of changes to the database:

1. Add a dead column to person that's like the one in pet.

2. Add a phone_number column to person.

3. Add a salary column to person that is float.

4. Add a dob column to both person and pet that is a DATETIME.

5. Add a purchased_on column to person_pet of type DATETIME.

6. Add a parent to pet column that's an INTEGER and holds the id for this pet's parent.

7. Update the existing database records with the new column data using UPDATE statements. Don't forget about the purchased_on column in the person_pet relation table to indicate when that person bought the pet.

8. Add four more people and five more pets, and assign their ownership and which pets are parents. On this last part remember that you get the id of the parent, then set it in the parent column.

9. Write a query that can find all the names of pets and their owners bought after 2004. The key to this is to map the person_pet based on the purchased_on column to the pet and parent.

10. Write a query that can find the pets that are children of a given pet. Again look at the pet.parent to do this. It's actually easy, so don't over think it.

11. Update your code.sql file you've been putting all the code in so that it uses the DROP TABLE IF EXISTS syntax.

12. Use ALTER TABLE to add height and weight columns to person and put that in your code.sql file.

13. Run your new code.sql script to reset your database, and you should have no errors.

You should do this by writing an ex13.sql file with these new things in it. You then test it by resetting the database using code.sql and then running ex13.sql to alter the database and run the SELECT queries that confirm you made the right changes.

Further Study

Continue reading the documentation for DROP TABLE (https://sqlite.org/lang_droptable.html) and ALTER TABLE (https://sqlite.org/lang_altertable.html) and then go to the SQLite3 language page at https://sqlite .org/lang.html and read the documentation for the remaining CREATE and DROP statements.

Using Python's Database API

P ython has a standardized database API that enables you to use the same code to access multiple databases. Each database you wish to connect to has a different module that knows how to talk to that database and follows the standard in PEP 249 (https://www.python.org/dev/peps/pep-0249/). This makes it easier to work with databases that all have different APIs for accessing them. For this exercise you'll be using the `sqlite3` module found at https://docs.python.org/2/library/sqlite3.html to work with SQL.

Learning an API

One thing you will *constantly* have to do as a programmer is learn APIs written by other people. I haven't specifically covered the most efficient way to do this because it's something that most programmers simply pick up by way of learning a language. The Python language and its modules are intertwined so closely that you can't help but learn the APIs in these modules when you learn Python. However, there is an efficient way that I use to learn APIs, and in this exercise you're going to learn it.

To learn an API like the `sqlite3` module I would do this:

1. Find all the documentation for the API, and if there is no documentation then find the code.

2. Review the samples or test code and replicate them in my own files. Reading them usually isn't enough. I will actually get them working because, guess what, many times the documentation doesn't work with the current version of the API. Making everything in the documentation work will help me find all the things they forgot to mention.

3. Take notes on any Works For Me (WFM) situations as I work on getting the sample code to work on my machine. A WFM is where the person writing the documentation left out significant configuration steps because their computer is already configured. Most programmers who write documentation don't start with a fresh machine, so they leave out libraries and software they installed that nobody else has. These WFM gaps will bite me later when I try to set up the API in production, so I note them for later.

4. Make flash cards or notes for all of the main API entry points and what they do.

5. Attempt to write a small test spike that uses the API but using only my notes. If I hit a part of the API I don't remember, I jump back to the documentation and update my notes.

6. Finally, if the API is difficult to use, I'll consider "wrapping" it with a simple API that does only the things I need so I can forget about it.

If doing this doesn't teach you the API, then you should consider finding a different one to use. If the author of the API tells you to "read the code," there is most likely another project that has documentation. Go use that project. If you must use this API, then consider taking your notes based on their code and writing a book that you sell to make money off the author's laziness.

Exercise Challenge

You are to study the `sqlite3` API in this way and then attempt to write your own database simplification API. Keep in mind that the DB API 2.0 is already a nice simple API for accessing a database, so you're only *practicing* having to wrap a terrible API. Your goal should be to learn the `sqlite3` API well enough to then devise a simpler way to access it.

Sometimes "simpler" is purely subjective or based on current needs. You could decide that what you need to simplify is not how to talk to a SQL database, but rather how *you* need to talk to a SQL database. If your application only needs to deal with people and pets then your simplification could simply be making an API that is only for you.

Further Study

Read the documentation for other database APIs in Python. You can read the Pyscopg PostgreSQL API (http://initd.org/psycopg/docs/) and the MySQL Python Driver (https://dev.mysql.com/doc/connector-python/en/).

Creating an ORM

The final exercise in the SQL part of the book is a big jump. You know the basics of the SQL language with one database. You also should be proficient with Python's OOP. It's now time to combine these two and create an object relational manager (ORM). An ORM's job is to take plain old Python classes and translate them into stored rows in a database's tables. If you've ever used Django, you've used their ORM to store your data. In this exercise you'll attempt to reverse engineer how to do that.

Exercise Challenge

In the real world if a programmer working for me asked to create their own ORM I'd say, "No way. Use an existing one." Work situations are different from educational situations because someone is paying you to get things working. You can't really justify using your work time to create things that honestly do not benefit your employer. However, your own personal time is all for you and, being a beginner, you should be attempting to re-create as many classic pieces of software as you can.

Creating an ORM will teach you about many problems related to the mismatch between object-oriented concepts and SQL. There are many things that SQL can model that classes tend to stumble on. There's also the problem that everything is a table in SQL. Attempting to create your own ORM will teach you so much about both SQL and OOP that I recommend spending a good amount of time crafting the best one you can.

Some key features you should have in your ORM include the following:

1. It should be safe to pass a string to your ORM from outside. If you are using f-strings to craft your SQL, you are doing it wrong. The reason is, if you do f"SELECT * FROM {table_name}, then someone can externally set table_name to SQL like person; DROP TABLE person. Your database will most likely run this and destroy everything or worse. Some databases even let you run system commands inside SQL. This is called a "SQL injection," and you should not have it in your ORM.

2. All the CRUD operations but in Python. I recommend you skip the CREATE TABLE portion until you get everything else to work. Simple INSERT, SELECT, UPDATE, and DELETE are easy to craft, but creating the scheme of a database from class definitions involves some major Python voodoo to really work. Use a hand-crafted .sql file to create your database, and then once you have everything else working you can attempt a scheme system to replace the .sql file.

3. Matching Python types to SQL types as well as new types to handle SQL types. You may find that you have to do some juggling to fit Python's data types into your SQL tables. Maybe that's too much of a pain so you end up making all your own data types. This is what Django did.

4. Transactions would be an advanced topic, but attempt it if you can get through this.

I'll also say that in this exercise you can steal features from as many projects as you like. Feel free to look at Django's ORM when working on your design. Finally, I highly recommend you start with *only* getting an ORM that works with the little database you created in this part of the book. Once you get something working with that database, you can then work on generalizing it to work with any database.

Further Study

As mentioned in the beginning of the book, *Joe Celko's SQL for Smarties, Fifth Edition* (Morgan Kaufmann, 2014), will teach you every single thing you ever need to know about SQL. Joe's books are excellent and will take you far beyond this tiny crash course.

PART VII
Final Projects

The final part of the book is where you step up to more advanced projects and try to nail down your personal process. These projects are a mix of difficulties, but they should help you formalize your process and figure out what is working well for you. The most important thing is that you should be on the path to analyzing how *you* work and what is best for you. Maybe you didn't do everything I suggest in this book regarding personal development, but I hope you continue to pick this book apart and find ways to analyze yourself. Doing this will give you an effective way to grow and improve as a programmer.

We should review what you've learned so far since you'll be asked to apply as much of it as you can:

- In Part I you got your start with some introductory material.

- In Part II you learned how to get hacking and how to make your start as smooth as possible.

- In Part III you learned about data structures and algorithms, but also learned how to focus on quality and write good tests.

- In Part IV you applied your testing and quality skills to projects focusing on test-driven development (TDD) and auditing.

- In Part V you learned about parsing, but also about measuring your quality as you work and writing effective tests.

- In Part VI you studied SQL databases and learned a new process for analyzing data and structuring it well.

In this part you will apply everything to a set of projects, making sure to focus on the three areas of improvement:

1. Process, by attempting to define your process and sticking to it

2. Quality, by focusing on automated testing, testing tools, and tracking your quality progress

3. Creativity, by trying to solve problems that are not too well defined and starting off with some loose fun hacking

What Is Your Process?

For this entire book I have dictated to you what process tools I want you to use. Each section I gave you a different challenge that focused on process, quality, or creativity and then gave you exercises to work on them. You've been tracking your quality and looking at graphs of what's working for you and what isn't. Now it's time for you to develop your own process for completing a project and then apply it to the projects in this section of the book.

Take the time to come up with your process theme. Is it hacking then TDD? Is it straight TDD all the time and lots of auditing? Is it just hacking and auditing? I don't mean to pick just two things, but you should think out your theme. Think of it as your personal style choice. I happen to like hats and red shirts. Don't ask me why, I just like them. That's what this process description is for you. It's your polka-dot dresses and yellow shoes on a summer day. In programming I generally follow the theme of, "hack, refine, test, break."

Once you have your simple theme statement, it's time to work out your steps for this theme. Write them down on a card so you can follow along with them, and I'll warn you that simpler is much better than complex. Complex processes are difficult to work on. Your process should also hit creativity and quality. My process is different for different projects, but I've taught you all of them throughout this book. Use what I've taught you so far to come up with your own.

Once you have your process laid out, go back through your notes and see if you can find metrics to justify what you've chosen. Maybe you've chosen TDD because it made you *feel* like you were writing more solid code, but then your quality metrics in Part V weren't really all that good. There's something to be said for using a process you like, but if the process you like isn't working it's time to toss it in the recycle bin.

With your process figured out, it's time to work on some projects to test it out. Don't be afraid to be wrong. Sometimes we think something we've decided is the best thing ever, and then the heat of battle melts it like an atom bomb. This is a science experiment for you, so if something is a total disaster then use your tracking and metrics to find out why and simply regroup to try again.

blog

Y ou should have your process theme written up as described in the beginning of this section, and you should have your process listed out and ready to go. To get started we'll make a totally new tool called `blog` as a warm-up for the rest of this section.

You should take this project slowly and try not to rush it. The goal is not to be a fast programmer. It's better to build speed fluidly and slowly by methodically going slow until how you work is simply second nature. If you always rush, then you'll be sloppy.

Make sure to keep your notebook handy and track facts and metrics about your work. You are trying to see if there's a process that will work for you as a method of working later. Not all methods work all the time, which is why I've tried to teach you various tactics and strategies for working that are used by many different programmers. If you do this project and you find out that something you did didn't work, then your notes will help you find out why. Change it up for the next project and see if something else works better.

Exercise Challenge

I'm tasking you with writing a simple command line blogging tool called `blog`. It's a very creative name for a very creative project. Blogs are some of the first projects early programmers write but your project is going to generate the blog locally and then send it to a server using another tool called `rsync`. Here's the requirements for this exercise:

1. If you don't know what a blog is then you should probably go start one and try it for a little while. There are plenty of platforms, but you might like either WordPress or Tumblr. Just use it for a little while and take notes on its features that you might want to copy. Don't go crazy.

2. You're going to want to learn how to use a templating system for styling your HTML pages. I recommend you use either the Mako (http://www.makotemplates.org/) or Jinja (http://jinja. pocoo.org/) template systems. These systems let you make template HTML files that you can then put the real content into based on text files the user has placed in a directory.

3. You'll want to use Markdown (https://pypi.python.org/pypi/Markdown) as your blogging format, so install the `markdown` library for your project.

4. Your blog will be a static file blog, so you'll want to use `python -m SimpleHTTPServer 8000` as demonstrated on the SimpleHTTPServer instructions (https://docs.python.org/2/library/ simplehttpserver.html). This will serve files to your browser out of the directory where you dump them.

5. You'll need a command line tool called `blog` to work with someone's blog.

6. Before you work, think through all of the things your `blog` tool has to do and then devise all the commands that are needed and their arguments. Then check out the docopt project (https://github.com/docopt/docopt) as a way to implement these commands.

7. You should use `mock` (https://pypi.python.org/pypi/mock) to mock out anything that you need to test, especially for error conditions. Watch the video for this exercise for a demonstration on using `mock`.

Other than that you are free to develop this `blog` tool how you want. Get creative. All that needs to happen is a blog is created somehow that I then can put on a server to be viewed.

Finally, the way I might put a blog like this online is with `rsync` using this command:

```
rsync —azv dist/* myserver.com:/var/www/myblog/
```

It's possible that this is a little more advanced, but this could be a good time to learn how to serve static files. There's a *Study Drill* that also talks about how to use Amazon S3 to do this.

Study Drills

1. Static files to your own server is fun and all, but wouldn't it be better if the `blog` tool worked with Amazon S3? There's a project called Boto3 (https://aws.amazon.com/sdk-for-python/) that will give you everything you need to make `blog` do this.

2. Write a `blog serve` command that uses the `SimpleHTTPServer` class to simply serve the blog directly rather than generating it separately.

bc

Y ou should be warmed up and ready to work on this new project. I'm usually assuming you would
do these projects over one or two days as two- to three-hour sessions, but you can typically take
as long as you need to implement them as much as you can.

This project is all about using what you learned in Part V to create the language for the bc program.
We already implemented the simple math for bc in Exercise 36 but now you're going to implement as
much of the bc language as you can. There are a large number of operators for bc as well as functions
and control structures. Your goal is to implement this in stages using what you learned about recursive
descent parsers.

I would focus heavily on building your parser in stages starting with scanning, then parsing, then analysis,
and using sample bc code to test it. This project could be massive since you're implementing a language
by hand, but complete as much of the syntax as you can.

Exercise Challenge

The bc language has the capability to do more than just process math. I never use more than just the
basic math, but the full language is rather powerful. You have the capabilities to define functions, use
if-statements, and implement many other common programming constructs. In your implementation
you will not be able to implement the entire bc language as it is simply too large. Instead, you should
implement just the following:

1. All the math operators

2. Variables

3. Functions

4. if-statements

This is actually the order you should probably implement the language. First, get the operators working
and parsing just fine. Feel free to steal the minimalist implementation you created in Exercise 35 to
get started. Once you have that, implement variables, which will require you to make your analyzer
properly handle the storing and retrieving of the variables. Finally, you can implement functions and then
if-statements.

You'll want to dig up any documentation on the GNU version of bc as that will have a nice complete
description of the language so you can implement it. There's nothing magical about it since they mostly
copied everything from C, and many other languages are similar to it.

As you work on this challenge take your time and do it in steps. The beauty of implementing a language is you can actually do it in a logical clean order going from scanning to parsing to analysis without much bouncing around between the three phases.

Finally, remember that you are implementing a recursive descent parser, and honestly just a baby version of real big time computer science parsing. If you are looking to do serious parsing work, then please use a parser generator rather than writing one by hand. Writing them by hand is merely a fun challenge and a way to learn how a parser logically structures the processing of text.

Study Drill

To study the bc language you should grab the source code to it from http://ftp.gnu.org/gnu/bc/ and look for the files bc.y, sbc.y, and scan.l. It may be confusing, so go research a tool called lex and one called yacc.

ed

If your process is working then you should be able to focus on one long project for a few weeks at a time. In this project your goal is to create the most accurate faithful copy of the ed command as you possibly can. The goal of this exercise is to not be creative at all but to do a methodical exact copy of another piece of software. Think of this as a forgery exercise. You'd want something so good that you could put it in place of the original ed and nobody would know.

This exercise will be to create a master copy of the ed command as exactly as you can, which means your test suite should run the real ed and your version against the same scripts to compare the output. This is like the master copy exercise you did when learning algorithms, except you're copying the behavior of an existing piece of software rather than trying to memorize it. The process is similar, but you get to use test suites to help make it go faster.

Exercise Challenge

The ed tool is one of the very first Unix text editors in existence, and frankly, it sucks. I actually can't imagine how anyone used ed to edit text as it is one of the most user-hostile pieces of software in existence. If you can't imagine how much computing sucked back in the bad old days of Unix, forging a copy of ed will give you a taste.

Something to realize about ed is that, while it does support scripting, it was originally used *interactively*. It was like a MUD for text files. You first ran ed and it started in a command mode that let you modify the text with commands. When you did a command that required input it would enter input mode until that command ended. You also had to know the addresses of lines to edit. This may seem like a pain but compared to other text editors at the time this was magic from a unicorn horn.

To complete your ed copy you'll need to rely heavily on the re library in Python (https://docs.python.org/ 2/library/re.html) to do your regular expressions. We used this library in Exercise 31, so you should be familiar with it and RegEx in general.

I also suggest you attempt to use ed for one 45-minute session to write some code for your ed project. The pain of doing this will teach you much about how to copy it.

Other than that, you will want to read the man ed page to get the basics of the command and possibly watch tutorials on using it. A good first step would be to find different example scripts you find online and try to make them work as your first test case.

WARNING! I'll give you a clue that you'll want to use a finite state machine to handle the modal nature of the ed command.

Study Drills

1. Find the source code to GNU ed and take a look, even if you don't know C.

2. Turn your ed implemenation into a module that you can then use in other projects. You'll need this for later exercises.

3. Never make a piece of software like this again unless you're just bored.

sed

You implemented a "baby version" of sed in Exercise 9 when you were learning how to make quick and dirty hacks. In this exercise you'll attempt another exact faithful copy of the command. In the *Study Drills* of Exercise 48 you were tasked with creating a module from your ed implementation. If you didn't do that, then you'll need to do this for your sed command and have sed use it.

How is your process working out? Are you finding that it's helping you on these longer projects? Are there things you think you need to change? Have you been collecting metrics or do you feel that you are past that now? Take the time before you start this exercise to look through your journal and see how much you've improved since you started the book.

The challenge for this exercise is to take code from the ed project in Exercise 48 and reuse it in this project. The concept of "reusability" is central to how software works, but many times planning for reuse in a project leads to disaster. Too often people design software so that every component can be used in other software, but in doing so they merely overcomplicate the design with no real plan to use anything in any other project. It's better to make software that is discrete and stands on its own, and *then* pull pieces out that you can use when *starting* another project.

I typically write my software with absolutely no concern for reusability. I do not care if parts of the project will be used in other projects. I only care that this one piece of software works well and has high quality. When I start a new project I'll go look at other things I've written and see if there's anything I can use again. If there is I spend the time in the older project to pull out the part I can use into a module. This makes my reuse process look like this:

1. Implement a fully working, high-quality piece of software with automated tests. Do not care about any part of it being used by any other software.

2. Start a new project that might use code from the other project.

3. Go back to the first project and pull the code out into a separate module, making this first project use it and *change absolutely nothing else*.

4. Once all the original automated tests run fine with the module in place in the original project, use the module in the new project.

5. Attempting to use the new module in the new project will find changes to make in the module. Make the changes and make sure they work with the original software as well.

You cannot do this without automated tests, so if your ed project didn't have tests I'm wondering if you've been reading this book or not. Go back and make sure you have full coverage of your ed project with your tests.

Exercise Challenge

First you'll want to pull out the parts of the ed project that handle the commands and put it in a module that ed uses without breaking the tests. This will honestly be one of the hardest parts of this project since sed mostly just uses those but without the modal nature of ed's interactive interface.

Next, you'll either want to grab your old code from Exercise 9 and dust it off or start over from scratch on this new project. Once you have that decided you'll begin by implementing as much of sed as possible using the ed module. The creativity in this exercise is deciding what exactly is necessary for both projects to use, then placing that in the module.

Your goal with this implementation is to make an exact and faithful copy of the sed comand. There is no creativity in this part of the exercise. Just try to be as meticulous as you possibly can and use automated testing to confirm that your command and the original sed work the same.

Finally, as you work on sed you'll find things you need in the module. You'll need to make the changes to the module, get them working in sed, then go back to ed and make them work there. This process of bouncing between three projects will be a challenge, so I suggest you keep to your 45-minute time chunks so you don't get burned out context switching.

Study Drill

As you worked on the module were there any coding habits you found made it difficult to pull the code out? What are they?

vi

I am going to prison for this exercise. You have a module that implements features used in both ed and sed. Obviously the next step is to implement the most hated and useful text editor in the history of the world: vi. If you knew Lisp you could implement Emacs, but nobody has time to create a whole new operating system pretending to be a text editor. Life is too short to hold down three keys and hit tab all day.

The goal of this exercise is *not* to do a dead accurate copy of vi. That's a very large project, but if you feel like trying it then go for it. Your goal in this project is to do one more reuse of your ed module and to play around with the Python curses module (https://docs.python.org/2/howto/curses.html). The curses module lets you do old-school text Terminal window and graphic manipulation. Actually "graphics" should be in quotes because there are very little actual graphics in curses.

You'll use curses to create a baby vi implementation that lets you open files, run ed and sed commands using your module, and use curses to display them to the Terminal screen. You'll also find out that attempting to automatically test this is going to be *very* difficult. You'll get extra points if you can figure out how to do a fake curses testing framework, but that's going to require some magical wizard skills with a Unix pty system (I think).

The better way to make this testable is to put as much of your vi into Python modules as possible so that you can test the code without having to run the curses screen system. When I say "modules" I don't really mean a fully baked Python module that you install with pip like you did with the ed module. I mean modules right in the code for the vi and then imported into your project.

The way to think of this project is to separate the code that controls the view (curses) from the rest of the code so that you can plug in your own fake view for the testing. That then leaves a small amount of functionality that you can test manually by actually running your vi.

Exercise Challenge

We will not be implementing all of vi. I need to really make this clear because actual vi is old and very complex, so doing a full master copy of it will take a long time. You are really only doing the following:

1. Take your ed module.

2. Create a curses UI to it.

3. Make it work on multiple files.

That's more or less all you're doing, so the first thing you should focus on is how curses works. Read the curses documentation to find out how it works and write as many test hacks as necessary to understand it.

Once you have a handle on `curses` you'll then need to learn how to use `vi`. I've included a `vi` crash course video for this exercise that you can watch, and there are a few `vi` cheat sheets online to reference. I suggest you watch my tutorial to `vi` and try to use the real `vi` to edit code during this session. You'll actually have a good idea of how `vi` works from your implementation of ed and `sed`. In theory, `vi` is just "visual ed," so you're mostly just giving ed a better UI.

Study Drills

1. How did the finite state machine from your ed implementation match up with the one you used in this `vi` implementation (assuming you used that design)?

2. How hard would it be to do a GUI version of this rather than `curses`? I don't recommend you do that, but research it and see what it'd take.

lessweb

We are nearing the end of the book, so I'm going to give you one project in the final two exercises. You are going to create a web server. In this exercise you simply learn about the Python `http.server` module and how to create a simple web server using it. You'll be given instructions and then expected to read the documentation to figure out how to do it. There won't be too much guidance as, by now, you should be able to do most everything on your own.

Once you've created your web server you will then write a set of tests to attempt to *hack* you web server. I'll give you some guidance on this in the *Breaking It* section, but by now you should be very comfortable in finding flaws in code you write.

Exercise Challenge

You'll need to read the Python 3 `http.server` documentation (https://docs.python.org/3/library/http.server.html) to start. You should also read the Python 3 `http.client` documentation (https://docs.python.org/3/library/http.client.html) as well as the documentation for `requests` (http://docs.python-requests.org/en/master/). You'll be using either `requests` or `http.client` to write tests for the `http.server` you create.

Next, your job is to create a web server using `http.server` that can do the following:

1. Be configured from a configuration file

2. Run continuously and handle requests it receives

3. Serve up files from configured directories

4. Respond to requests for websites and serve the correct content

5. Log all requests coming in to a file to read later

If you read the example in the documentation you can probably get most of this working in a basic way. Part of this exercise is how to hack a naïve web server, so you should just get it barely working and then we'll move to the next part.

Breaking It

Your job in this section is to attack your web server any way you can. You can start with the OWASP Top 10 Vulnerabilities list (https://www.owasp.org/index.php/Category:OWASP_Top_Ten_Project) and then move on to other common attacks. You will also want to read the Python 3 `os` module documentation (https://docs.python.org/3/library/os.html) to implement some of the fixes. Here's an additional list of mistakes I'm positive you'll make:

1. Unwanted directory traversal. You are probably taking the basic path from the URL (`/some/file/index.html`) and simply opening it as requested. Maybe you're adding the full path of the file on the OS (`/Users/zed/web/some/file/index.html`) and think you're good. Try accessing a file outside this directory by using `..` path specifiers. If you can request `/../../../../../../../../etc/passwd` then you win. Try to explain why this happens and what can you do to fix it.

2. Not handling unwanted requests. You most likely look for `GET` and `POST`, but what happens if someone does `HEAD` or `OPTIONS`?

3. Sending a giant HTTP header. See if you can make the Python `http.server` explode or slow down by sending it a really large HTTP request header.

4. Not raising an error when an unknown domain is requested. Some people take it as a feature (cough, Nginx) that a "random" website is served when the server doesn't recognize the domain. Your server should be white list only, and if it doesn't recognize the domain it should give a 404 error.

These are just a few of the small mistakes people make. Study as many others as you can, and then write automated tests for your server to demonstrate them before you fix them. If you can't find any of these errors in your server, then *create them on purpose*. It's also instructive to learn how these errors are made.

Study Drills

1. Read about the `os.chroot` function in the Python 3 `os` documentation.

2. Research how you would use that function and other `os` module functions to create a "chroot jail."

3. Using as many of the functions in `os`, and any modules you can find, rewrite your server to properly chroot jail and drop privileges to a safe user (not root). On `Windows` this may be very difficult, so either try it out on a Linux computer or just skip this entirely.

moreweb

N ow that you've created a web server using the Python `http.server` library you can move to the very final project. You are going to create your own web server from abolute nothing using everything you've learned so far. In Exercise 51 you created the majority of the handling that is "above" the `http.server` module. You didn't do any network connection handling or HTTP protocol parsing. In this final exercise you will implement all the gear necessary to replicate what `http.server` does for your `lessweb` server.

Exercise Challenge

To complete this exercise you'll want to read about the Python 3 `asyncio` module (https://docs.python. org/3/library/asyncio.html). This library provides you with tools for handling socket requests, creating servers, waiting for signals, and most everything else you'll need. If you want an extra challenge doing this, then you can use the Python 3 `select` module (https://docs.python.org/3/library/select.html), which provides an even lower level for handling sockets. You should use this documentation to create a series of small little socket servers and clients.

Once you understand how to create servers and clients that talk over a TCP/IP socket you'll need to move to processing HTTP requests. This part of the project is going to be daunting as the HTTP standard is insane and way more complicated than it needs to be. I would start with the simplest HTTP parsing library you can design, and then expand on it with more and more samples. The first place to start is the RFC 7230 (https://tools.ietf.org/html/rfc7230), but be prepared to experience some of the worst writing humans could devise.

The best way to study RFC 7230 is to first extract out all of the grammar listed in the Collected ABNF appendix (https://tools.ietf.org/html/rfc7230#appendix-B). At first glance this seems crazy since this is just a huge grammar specification. You actually learned how to read these in Part V of this book but on a smaller scale. You know how regular expressions, scanners, and parsers work and how to read a grammar like this. All you need to do is study this grammar and implement it a little bit at a time. When implementing this I would completely ignore any of the "chunk" grammar.

Once you've studied this grammar you should start writing a parser for HTTP using what you have already created. Use your data structures, parsing tools, and everything you can to create a valid parser for a small subset of HTTP. Try to cover as much of this grammar as you can. To help you out, there is a set of test files that have valid HTTP requests in them at https://learncodethehardway.org/more-python-book/ http_tests.zip. You can download this set of test cases and run them through your parser to confirm it works. I extracted many of these test cases from the *excellent* And-HTTP server (http://www.and.org/and-httpd/) and then augmented them with more basic examples. Your goal is to get as many of these as possible passing.

Finally, once you have a way to write a decent `asyncio` or `select` socket server and a way to parse HTTP, you can then put the two together and make your first functioning web server.

Breaking It

You should definitely try to break this web server, but you should also try something different here. You've written a parser for HTTP that tries to handle valid HTTP in the most logical way possible using an RDP-style parser. There's a good chance that your parser blocks many bad HTTP requests, so find some past attacks and try them on your web server. There are several website hacking automation tools out there, so grab one and point it at your server. Be safe about this, though, and make sure you are only running reputable testing tools and only on your own server.

Further Study

If you wanted to completely understand web servers and technology then use your `moreweb` server to create a web framework. I would suggest creating a website first and then extract the patterns you needed out of it for a web framework. The goal of such a framework is to encapsulate patterns that you use so that you can simplify later web applications you make. As with the `lessweb` and `moreweb` exercises, your goal should also be to research, implement, and exploit common attacks to web frameworks.

If you want to dive deep into TCP/IP I recommend the book *Effective TCP/IP Programming* by Jon C. Snader (Addison-Wesley, 2000). This book is written in C, but it is effectively "Learn TCP/IP the Hard Way" and covers 44 topics with simple code for you to understand how basic TCP/IP works. C is where TCP/IP was born, so much of how other languages handle socket connections seems weird until you know how C does it. By studying this you'll get a firm grounding in how socket servers work. The only warning is the book is a little dated, so the code should work, but it won't be the most modern code possible.

Index

Register Your Product at informit.com/register

Access additional benefits and **save 35%** on your next purchase

- Automatically receive a coupon for 35% off your next purchase, valid for 30 days. Look for your code in your InformIT cart or the Manage Codes section of your account page.
- Download available product updates.
- Access bonus material if available.
- Check the box to hear from us and receive exclusive offers on new editions and related products.

InformIT.com—The Trusted Technology Learning Source

InformIT is the online home of information technology brands at Pearson, the world's foremost education company. At InformIT.com, you can:

- Shop our books, eBooks, software, and video training
- Take advantage of our special offers and promotions (informit.com/promotions)
- Sign up for special offers and content newsletter (informit.com/newsletters)
- Access thousands of free chapters and video lessons

Connect with InformIT—Visit informit.com/community

the trusted technology learning source

Addison-Wesley · Adobe Press · Cisco Press · Microsoft Press · Pearson IT Certification · Prentice Hall · Que · Sams · Peachpit Press

 Pearson